The secret of life is enjoying the passage of time.

JAMES TAYLOR, "SECRET O' LIFE"

GREETINGS *from* KNIT CAFE

Suzan Mischer

Photographs by Victoria Pearson

STC CRAFT | A MELANIE FALICK BOOK
STEWART, TABORI & CHANG | NEW YORK

Published in 2009 by Stewart, Tabori & Chang
An imprint of Harry N. Abrams, Inc.

Originally published in hardcover in 2006 by Stewart, Tabori & Chang

Text copyright © 2006 by Suzan Mischer
All photographs except pages 13 and 144 copyright © 2006 by Victoria Pearson
Photographs pages 13 and 144 copyright © 2006 by Judy Gigliotti
Hand Made page 87 copyright © 2006 by Hope Anita Smith
Hope Anita Smith is the author of *The Way A Door Closes* (Henry Holt, 2003)

"Knitcafe" is a registered trademark of Knitcafe, Inc. and cannot be used
without the written permission of Knitcafe, Inc.

Library of Congress Cataloging-in-Publication Data:
Mischer, Suzan.
Greetings from knit cafe / Suzan Mischer ; photographs by Victoria Pearson.
p. cm.
Includes index.
ISBN 978-1-58479-768-5
1. Knitting--Patterns. 2. Knitwear. I. Title.
TT825.M58 2006
746.43'2--dc22
2005029383

Editor: Melanie Falick
Designer: Sarah Von Dreele
Production Manager: Jacqueline Poirier

The text of this book was composed in Avenir, Sabon, and Corky

Printed and bound in China
10 9 8 7 6 5 4 3 2 1

harry n. abrams, inc.
a subsidiary of La Martinière Groupe

115 West 18th Street
New York, NY 10011
www.hnabooks.com

For my family:

Gram & Grampa Kolb
Gram & Grandpa Reed
Dad & Gloria
Mom & Marty
Chuck, Doug, Britt & Craig
My Big Girls, Jenny & Heather
My Children, Charlie & Lilly
Brownie and Don

Whoever I am today
is because of you.

Love,
Suzan

contents

Pilates instructor, entertainment executive, surfer, psychiatrist, school teacher, minister, surgeon, mountain biker, stay-at-home mom (and dad), actor, actress, acupuncturist, yoga instructor, professional football player, symphony violinist, amazing kids of all ages, ER nurse, handwriting analyst, painter, makeup artist, chef, poet, judge, jewelry designer, entrepreneur...and on and on.

These are the people I get to hang out with EVERY DAY! They are the knitters who come to my store. They are what make Knit Cafe so much fun.

When I opened Knit Cafe, I was creating a place for me. I wanted a space where I could do many of my favorite things—listen to music, drink tea, play with wonderful yarns, think up fun ideas to knit and crochet, and meet new people. It quickly became "casa" to the entire neighborhood.

Welcome! Here is the story of how Knit Cafe came to be and what it has come to mean to me.

STARTING AT THE *VERY* BEGINNING

My earliest memories of knitting are back in my grandparents' living room in Williamsport, Pennsylvania. Grandma Kolb is sitting in her recliner beside Grandpa Kolb's recliner, her "close-up" glasses snug on her face. From time to time, she looks up and takes a sip of her highball or a drag on her cigarette, both of which rest on a table nearby, but otherwise, she is completely absorbed in her knitting, usually an intricately cabled fisherman-style sweater. Knitting is what Grandma Kolb did to unwind after a day of fishing or hunting with my grandfather. They were avid outdoorspeople. Her knitting bag was always next to her recliner and her pad of paper with her project notes on the table. I knew never to touch them.

When I was seven years old, Gram decided I was ready to learn how to knit. She gave me a pair of her long metal needles and some bright pink scratchy wool and began to teach me the basic knit stitch. My first project was a headband. I have vivid memories of taking my place in Grandpa's recliner and working quietly on that holey pink strip. I also remember how good it felt when Gram would look over and smile at me—as good as it felt when my mom taught me how to iron my dad's shirts and nodded her approval as I finished my first one! Being an antsy kid, I didn't stick with knitting consistently, but I did take my yarn and needles with me whenever I visited my grandparents.

When I was sixteen, Gram took me into her kitchen and excitedly pulled out a sweater she had made for me. It was knit out of heavy gray, black, and white Icelandic wool, the kind water can barely penetrate. It was from a pattern by Elizabeth Zimmermann and knit completely in the round. No seams! She was so impressed with the genius of this "new" concept in knitting. I liked the sweater very much and I thanked her over and over, even though secretly I wished it had been fluffy pink angora or something else more girlish. But I ended up wearing it all the time during cold, snowy winters. In fact, I STILL wear it. I take it with me skiing every year! (And that's me in it in the photo on the back flap of this book.) Today, I fully appreciate the mastery that my grandmother put into that sweater. And I'm grateful to her for planting the seeds in me all those years ago that have now grown into such a huge part of my life.

HEADING WEST

When I was in my 20s, I moved from from New Jersey to California (to be with a guy—what else?!). For a while I did office work for different companies but, ultimately, ended up at CBS Television Network. I started as a temp but worked my way into a permanent position and went on to become the vice president of specials and documentaries. This was an exciting time in my life. I was pretty independent, very busy, always in the middle of exciting things with exciting people. I was used to producers, directors, and writers calling me daily and feeling like I was on the inside track. I knit a bit during this time and I enjoyed it, but I definitely remained a novice, which was fine with me.

It wasn't until the early 1990s, after leaving CBS to be home with my kids, that I became an avid knitter. I loved being home and taking care of my family but shifting from the professional world to the stay-at-home mom world was tough for me—the change in priorities and pace and the loss of the social network took me a while to get used to. Eventually I found a lot of comfort in my knitting and enjoyed teaching myself new techniques and trying new projects. I carried my knitting with me everywhere and I began to notice how friendly people were toward me when they saw it. It had been similar when I was pregnant—a baby-filled belly and a knitting bag seemed to evoke the same ease. One day, I was walking down Rodeo Drive in Beverly Hills, my knitting stuffed in my purse, when a nice old man stopped me and told me all about his mother and the wonderful things she used to knit for him. He seemed so happy to be able to talk about his mom with someone. I was still pretty lonely and I really enjoyed the pleasant exchanges my knitting provoked.

When I started to drive my children to school in the morning, I would stop at my local Starbucks on my way home to have some tea and knit. It was one of those places where customers work on their computers and read newspapers for hours and moms gather and chat while their kids run all over the place. Every day I saw the same people and came to know them. I enjoyed my time there but kept thinking how perfect it would be if they had a yarn department. And then it struck me that I could create such a place, a place with great yarn, coffee and

tea, music and books, and comfortable welcoming chairs where people could relax! I started talking about my idea and, of course, some people thought I was crazy. Knitting is so uncool," they'd exclaim. "You can't make any money selling balls of yarn." But I was unfazed.

I had CBS stock stashed away, which felt like just the right financial cushion I needed to start my new endeavor. How perfect that my previous career could in some way help to launch this new one! I bandied around many ideas for names until, finally, Knit Cafe popped into my brain. It felt right immediately, so I contacted a lawyer, who helped me to trademark and register it. Once that was done, I felt like there was no turning back, so I called Sasha Emerson, an old friend who had left a career in the television industry to become an interior designer. Though I hadn't seen her in years, I had been following her work in books and magazines and was attracted to her quirky, colorful sense of design. I told her my vision—I had by

this time filled a journal with ideas about the types of yarn and other merchandise I wanted to carry, beverages to offer, furnishings, color schemes, and the laid-back community vibe I wanted to create—and we began on the biggest hoot you can imagine. It was so much fun putting it all together.

MOVING IN

I knew I wanted to be in West Hollywood, an eclectic neighborhood I had come to love while working at CBS, and was lucky to find a charming old space on Melrose Avenue surrounded by really good restaurants, chic boutiques, and interior design showrooms. Just four blocks from the famed Sunset Boulevard, up the street from The Improv comedy club, around the corner from a little theater, and across the street from a progressive elementary school, the 900-square-foot skylit space—formerly an antiques store— was perfect, give or take a few renovations.

Sasha combed flea markets and vintage furniture shops and found a treasure trove of choices, including an amazing collection of circa 1950s Thaden-Jordon furniture that was once used in a German school. We reupholstered chairs in lime green fur and bright red and orange Sunbrella striped fabrics and covered benches in crazy quilts. Sasha gathered wonderful vintage California pottery and hand-painted lamps made out of Moroccan camel udders (really!). We chose a bold, bright floral-like wallpaper for one of the walls and commissioned how-to-knit pastel drawings by local artist Peter Tigler and beautiful photos of flowers and knitting needles by photographer Judy Gigliotti. We put two work tables in the store—one in front and one in back—and in the center, we had a blond wood beverage bar built and arranged comfortable chairs around a coffee table for relaxing and knitting. For yarn, we had floor-to-ceiling shelving built along an entire wall.

My theory for choosing the yarn and other merchandise for the store was to start with what I love. That meant lots of bright colors. In fact, it wasn't until after I had just about everything in stock and arranged that I realized that I had actually forgotten to order white and black yarn, a mistake I rectified quickly. In addition to stocking all of the necessary tools and an extensive selection of books, Sasha and I designed tote bags and roll-up needle cases using vintage fabrics and then found seamstresses who continue to make them for me to sell to this day. Start to finish, it took about four months to get Knit Cafe ready.

After dropping off my children at school in the morning, I would stop at my local Starbucks to have some tea and knit. I kept thinking how perfect it would be if Starbucks had a yarn department. And then it struck me that I could create such a place—with great yarn, coffee and tea, music and books, and comfortable, welcoming chairs where people could relax.

DOORS OPEN!

On the morning of July 1, 2002, I arranged a large bouquet of multicolored roses in a vase in the center of the store, slipped my favorite Norah Jones CD into the audio system, and officially opened Knit Cafe for business. One by one all of my neighbors stopped by to welcome me and share a cup of coffee. Friends sent more flowers and local knitters walked in with smiles on their faces, happy to have a yarn shop in their neighborhood. I was so excited when I made my first sale—a pair of bamboo needles—that I called home to tell my family and I still have the first dollar I earned in a special box of personal mementos along with the kids' baby teeth. Two weeks later I hired my first employee and gradually I figured out the computerized inventory system and most of the other systems that keep the store running smoothly. One of the biggest—and best—surprises in those early days was my relationship with the private school across the street. Very soon after we opened the art teacher asked if she could bring in her students to draw in the store and, before I knew it, students were hanging out and knitting after school, begging their parents to come in, too.

DAY TO DAY

Knit Cafe has always been open seven days a week, 10:30AM to 8:30PM, and on most days there's a class or group gathering going on. On Tuesday night, we offer Project Class. Each week we choose a different small project, such as a baby sweater, mittens, a cabled scarf, or a felted bag, and everyone who signs up works on their own version of it. On Wednesday night we give beginner lessons. Thursday night Group Therapy is probably my favorite weekly activity. About twenty of us gather for two to three hours of talking and knitting. We talk about everything—from men to menopause to gossip to books. A few times we have tried to become a book club too, but we've never been able to agree on a book to read. At least a few people always bring food and I provide the beverages. It has become tradition that, at the end of the night, I ask a random, sometimes obscure knitting question (see Stump the Knitter on page 45) and whoever gets the correct answer first wins a ball of yarn or a used book donated from the personal stash of the previous week's winner. My favorite questions involve math and don't allow for the use of a calculator (really keeps everyone on their toes).

Next we have Tabloid Friday. This activity began without any planning when Mimi, who works on Fridays, began bringing in her celebrity magazines to read. Before I knew it, customers were coming in throughout the day to read her copies (probably feeling less guilty about indulging because they weren't actually buying them) and to talk to her and each other about who was doing what to whom.

On Saturday mornings we have Kids' Club, which is open to any kids who already know the basics. We work on a different project every month, such as the Kids' Club Favorite Skirt (page 70), dolls, and sweaters. One or two Saturdays a year I also plan a Family Day. For this event, I encourage customers to bring in a family member with whom they'd like to hang out and knit. I also invite everyone who comes to knit a square for a blanket. Staff members sew the blanket together and then we donate it to a family in need.

We don't usually have specific activities scheduled for Sundays, but it's always a nice time to be at Knit Cafe. The mood is especially mellow and people wander in casually, often after they've shopped at the farmer's market around the corner or had tea and a scone at the bakery across the street. Before I was a shop owner, I found it frustrating that most knitting stores weren't open on Sundays—it was usually the only day that I had to myself and I would have given anything to bask in bundles of yarn and pattern books—so keeping Knit Cafe open on Sundays has always been a priority for me.

I see Knit Cafe as a huge potluck! Everyone brings something to the table...good stories, good ideas, good food, good gossip, good advice, good news. It gives me infinite pleasure to watch the eclectic combinations of people and situations. It makes life funny.

knit cafe '06
all the things I love

The hilarious juxtaposition of different personalities. HOW PEOPLE WHO ARE SO DIFFERENT BECOME TRULY GOOD FRIENDS. How much everyone loves to be together. WHEN SOMEONE CALLS FROM AN INTERNATIONAL LOCATION TO SAY THEY WON'T BE COMING TO GROUP THERAPY THIS WEEK BECAUSE THEY ARE ON VACATION...DUH. When someone calls when they are sick to say they are sick and won't be in. WHEN SOMEONE CALLS FROM THE DELIVERY ROOM TO SAY SHE HAD HER BABY. How pissed off the whole group gets when someone has been abused by their boss, or kids, or in-laws, whomever. HOW PEOPLE LOOK FORWARD TO GETTING TO THE STORE SO THEY CAN DISCUSS AND WORK OUT A PROBLEM. How good it feels when the kids finish another project. HOW GOOD IT FEELS WHEN ANYBODY FINISHES ANOTHER PROJECT. Watching a husband sitting with a newspaper and a cup of coffee while his wife is off in Knitting Lala Land. WATCHING DADS HELP THEIR KIDS PICK OUT YARN. THEY OFTEN COME IN VERY RUSHED, BUT USUALLY LEAVE SMILING AND CONNECTED TO THEIR KIDS. Observing the similarities in all of us in justifying our yarn purchases. WHEN THE GUY WHO SERVICES THE CAPPUCCINO MACHINE CHECKS WITH HIS MOTHER TO SEE IF SHE NEEDS ANY YARN BEFORE HE LEAVES THE STORE.

HERE WE ARE

Knit Cafe is constantly changing, and each day has its own cast of characters. I'm no longer surprised (but I am always delighted) when I walk in and see people I'd never expect to even know each other engrossed in conversation, like a man wearing a dress discussing cooking tips with a Russian grandmother and a young film student. I have regular daytime customers and nighttime customers, and those who only turn up on the weekends. Sometimes I actually forget (for a minute) that Knit Cafe is my store. Customers help customers, change the music on the CD player, and have even been known to sign the delivery slip for Joe, our UPS guy. So many people hang their hats here and leave bits and pieces of themselves (and their knitting) behind. Sometimes customers need me to remind them how to do an ssk or help them settle on a new project or pick up 320 dropped stitches. Or sometimes they just need me to be a good listener.

One of my main goals is for my customers to experience Knit Cafe as a refuge from the other pressures of their lives. I am not a perfectionist by nature but for a long time I worked in an environment where mistakes were very costly and people who made them were looked at critically. So I find great comfort and joy in having a place of work now where I and everyone else can make mistakes without gigantic consequences, where some mistakes can even bring on huge belly laughs.

If someone had told me twelve years ago, while I was sitting in a production truck with a headset on, trying to get the live broadcast of the Grammy Awards off the air on time, that I would one day be the happy, relaxed owner of a knitting store, I would never have believed it. But here I am.

For me, it's not just knitting, but "the world of knitting" that I am hopelessly drawn to. What I mean is that, for sure I enjoy the magic of creating with needles and yarn, but even more, I'm in love with being around knitters and knitting and yarn and ideas and camaraderie and life—and all of that comes in and out of the door of Knit Cafe every day.

Greetings!

the patterns

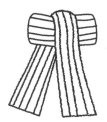

ARCHITECT SCARF

One day, a new knitter named Nicole (or Nicoli, as I have come to call her) walked into Knit Cafe with a friend. She had generously offered to make him a scarf. Being an architect and knowing EXACTLY what he wanted his scarf to look like, he presented her with a professional drawing done to scale that included every detail he envisioned. It was brilliant! I was so impressed, I asked if I could have a copy of the drawing for the store. Here is my interpretation of his drawing. I have to say that the guys who come into Knit Cafe seem to really like this scarf.

FINISHED MEASUREMENTS
Approximately 9½" wide by 80" long

YARN
Manos del Uruguay (100% handspun kettle-dyed wool; 135 yds / 100 g): 2 skeins each #04 blue (A) and #E green (B); 1 skein each #69 red (C) and #58 yellow (D)

NEEDLES
One pair size US 11 (8 mm) needles

Change needle size if necessary to obtain correct gauge.

NOTIONS
Yarn needle

GAUGE
18 sts and 16 rows = 4" (10 cm) in k2, p2 rib

NOTES

*K2, P2 RIB
Row 1: (RS) *K2, p2; repeat from * across to last 2 sts, k2
Row 2: P2, *k2, p2; rep from * across. Repeat Rows 1 and 2 for k2, p2 rib.

STRIPE SEQUENCE
Work 60 rows A, 64 rows B, 2 rows C, 18 rows A, 24 rows B, 6 rows D, 56 rows B, 2 rows C, 40 rows D, 32 rows A, 2 rows C, 14 rows B.

With A, CO 38 sts. Beg k2, p2 rib and Stripe Sequence. Work even until Stripe Sequence is complete. BO all sts in rib pattern. Using yarn needle, weave in all loose ends.

BERET
KAT COYLE

This beret is so easy to knit. Once the ribbed band is complete and the markers are placed so you know when to work the shaping, it's smooth sailing—in Stockinette stitch—all the way through. I feel like I've knit this beret a million different ways with all kinds of colors and yarns. Just be sure to use a yarn that gets the gauge the pattern calls for, that is, 6 stitches to the inch. Embellishments are always fun to add. Amira (see right) put a pretty felted flower on her beret.

FINISHED MEASUREMENTS
To fit average adult-sized head

Finished circumference: 18½"

YARN
Blue Sky Alpaca and Silk (50% super fine alpaca / 50% silk; 144 yards / 50 grams): 1 skein #133 light pink

NEEDLES
One 16" circular (circ) needle size US 4 (3.5 mm)

One set of five double-pointed needles (dpn) size US 4 (3.5 mm)

Change needle size if necessary to obtain correct gauge.

NOTIONS
8 stitch markers (one in a contrast color to mark end of rounds); yarn needle

GAUGE
24 sts and 31 rows = 4" in Stockinette stitch (St st)

BAND
Using circ needle, CO 112 sts. Join for working in the rnd being careful not to twist sts; place marker (pm) for beginning of rnd.

Rnds 1–6: *K2, p2; repeat from * around.

RISE
Rnd 7, Increase Rnd: *K14, m1, pm; rep from * around to last 14 sts, k14, m1 – 120 sts.
Rnd 8: Knit.
Rnd 9, Increase Rnd: *K15, m1; rep from * around – 128 sts.

Rnd 10: Knit.
Rnds 11–26: Continue to increase in this manner, working 1 more st between each marker every other round 8 more times, and working 1 knit rnd after each increase rnd – 192 sts.

CROWN
Note: Change to dpn when necessary for number of sts remaining.

Rnd 27, Decrease Rnd: *K22, k2tog; rep from * around – 184 sts remain.
Rnd 28: Knit.
Rnd 29, Decrease Rnd: *K21, k2tog; rep from * around – 176 sts remain.

Rnd 30: Knit.
Rnds 31–70: Continue to decrease in this manner, working 1 less st between each marker every other round 20 more times, and working 1 knit rnd after each decrease rnd – 16 sts remain.
Rnd 71: *K2tog; rep from * around – 8 sts remain.

FINISHING
Break off yarn, leaving several inches. Using yarn needle, thread yarn through remaining sts twice, draw tight and secure on WS. Using yarn needle, weave in all loose ends.

BOXER SHORTS
TERRI CUPERJIA

Once at our Thursday Night Group Therapy

gathering, we had a really fun conversation about mens' underwear—boxers vs. briefs. Most of us preferred boxers. We also agreed that boxers are the men's garments we are most likely to borrow. Right then, the idea for theses boxers was hatched! They are designed to have a nice relaxed fit through the legs.

FINISHED MEASUREMENTS
To fit Small (Medium, Large, X-Large)

Waist (before elastic): 37¾ (42¼ , 45, 46½)"
Hip: Approximately 44½ (49¾ , 52¾ , 54½)"

Sample shown in size Small

YARN
Twisted Sisters Mirage (52% rayon / 48% cotton; 140 yards / 50 grams): 5 (5, 6, 6) balls indigo (MC); 2 (2, 2, 3) balls natural (CC)

NEEDLES
One 20" circular (circ) needle size US 2 (3 mm)

One 20" circular needle size US 3 (3.25 mm)

Change needle size if necessary to obtain correct gauge.

NOTIONS
Crochet hook size D/3 (3.25 mm)

Smooth waste yarn; stitch markers; yarn needle; approximately 1½ (1½, 1¾, 1¾) yards ⅜" flat elastic

GAUGE
27 sts and 35 rows = 4" (10 cm) in Stockinette stitch (St st) using larger needles

NOTE
The Boxer Shorts are made in two pieces: Right Front/Back and Left Front/Back. They are worked from the top down, then the Waistband is worked from the Provisional CO edge up.

RIGHT FRONT/BACK
Using crochet hook, waste yarn and Provisional CO Method (see Special Techniques, page 138), CO 146 (164, 174, 180) sts. (RS) Change to larger circ needle, MC and St st; work 12 (10, 10, 10) rows even, ending with a WS row.

Shape Center Front and Back: (RS) Increase 1 st at beginning of this row, then every 16 rows twice, every 6 rows twice, every other row 2 (3, 3, 4) times, as follows: Work 2 sts, m1, work to end – 154 (172, 182, 189) sts. Work 3 (1, 1, 1) row(s) even, ending with a WS row.

Next Row: (RS) Increase 1 st at each side on this row, then every other row 1 (2, 2, 2) time(s), as follows: Work 2 sts, m1, work across to last 2 sts, m1, work 2 sts – 158 (178, 188, 195) sts.

***Next Row:** (WS) Increase 1 st on this row, as follows: Work to last 2 sts, m1-p, work 2 sts.

Next Row: (RS) Work 2 sts, m1, work across to last 2 sts, m1, work 2 sts – 161 (181, 193, 198) sts. Repeat from * 1 (2, 3, 3) time(s) – 164 (187, 200, 207) sts.

Next Row: (WS) Increase 2 sts on this row as follows: Work 2 sts, m1-p, work across to last 2 sts, m1-p, work 2 sts.

Next Row: (RS) Work 2 sts, m1, work across to last 2 sts, m1, work 2 sts – 168 (191, 204, 211) sts.

Next Row: (WS) Using Cable Cast On Method (see Special Techniques, page 137), CO 7 sts for the Front Crotch, work to end.

Next Row: (RS) CO 10 (11, 12, 12) sts for the Back Crotch, work to end – 185 (209, 223, 230) sts.

Work 39 (39, 41, 39) rows even, ending with a RS row.

Next Row: (WS) K2, purl across to last 2 sts, k2. Work 2 rows even, end with a WS row. BO all sts purlwise.

LEFT FRONT/BACK

Work as for Right Front/Back, reversing all shaping.

FINISHING

Sew center front and back seams, including the crotch; sew leg seams. Using yarn needle, weave in all ends. Block pieces to measurements.

Waistband:

Note: The Waistband is double-knit in rnds. This means that you will be knitting the RS and WS of the band simultaneously. By working the RS and WS together on Rnds 8, 16, and 24, you will create a casing for the elastic.

Beginning at center back, remove waste yarn and place all sts from Left/Front Back and Right Front/Back on smaller circ needle – 292 (328, 348, 360) sts. Join for working in the round, place marker (pm) for beginning of rnd.

Rnd 1: Using CC, k2tog, yo, [k1, yo] 21 (15, 16, 9) times, k2tog, yo; *[k1, yo] 22 (16, 17, 12) times, k2tog, yo*; repeat

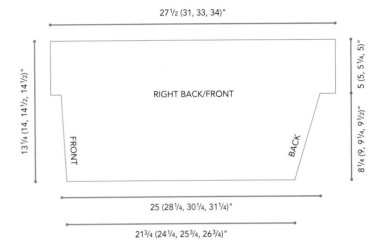

from * to * 3 (6, 6, 10) times; [k1, yo] 21 (15, 17, 9) times, k2tog, yo, ssk, yo, k2tog, yo, [k1, yo] 21 (15, 16, 9) times, k2tog, yo; *[k1, yo] 22 (16, 17, 12) times, k2tog, yo*; repeat from * to * 3 (6, 6, 10) times; [k1, yo] 21 (15, 17, 9) times, k2tog, yo, ssk, yo – 552 (612, 652, 660) sts.

Rnd 2: Slip all knit sts purlwise wyib, purl all yo's tbl.

Rnd 3: Slip all purl sts purlwise wyif, knit all knit sts.

Rnd 4: Slip all knit sts purlwise wyib, purl all purl sts.

Rnds 5 and 7: Repeat Rnd 3.

Rnd 6: Repeat Rnd 4.

Rnd 8: *Ssk; repeat from * around – 276 (306, 326, 330) sts remain.

Size S: Rnd 9: *[K1, yo] 21 times, k2tog, yo*; rep from * to * 11 times – 528 sts.

Size M: Rnd 9: K2tog, yo, *[k1, yo] 16 times, k2tog, yo*; repeat from * to * 15 times, [k1, yo] 14 times, k2tog, yo – 576 sts.

Size L: Rnd 9: K2tog, yo, [k1, yo] 22 times, k2tog, yo *[k1, yo] 23 times, k2tog, yo*; rep from * to * 11 times – 624 sts.

Size XL: Rnd 9: K2tog, yo, [k1, yo] 11 times, k2tog, yo *[k1, yo] 23 times, k2tog, yo*; rep from * to * 11 times, k2tog, yo, [k1, yo] 11 times, k2tog, yo – 628 sts.

All Sizes: Rnd 10: Repeat Rnd 2.

Rnds 11, 13, and 15: Repeat Rnd 3.

Rnds 12 and 14: Repeat Rnd 4.

Rnd 16: Repeat Rnd 8 – 264 (288, 312, 314) sts remain.

Rnd 17: *K1, yo; repeat from * around – 528 (576, 624, 628) sts.

Rnd 18: Repeat Rnd 2.

Rnds 19, 21, and 23: Repeat Rnd 3.

Rnds 20 and 22: Repeat Rnd 4.

Rnd 24: Ssk, *ssk, BO 1 st purlwise; repeat from * around.

Measure around your waist and subtract 4"; cut two pieces of elastic to this length. Thread one piece of elastic through the bottom casing and secure the ends. Thread the second piece of elastic through the top casing and secure the ends. Block garment lightly.

CANYON HIKING SOCKS
JULIA TRICE

In California, we have so many great trails

to take hikes and long walks on with our dogs or family and friends. From Knit Cafe, which is in the heart of urban West Hollywood, I can drive to a hiking trail within five to ten minutes depending on traffic. These knee-high socks are super-comfortable thanks to the shaping along the calf—and are great for protecting legs from bugs and thorns. When not hiking, I also like them with a casual skirt.

SIZES
Small (Medium, Large)
To fit US woman's shoe size 5-6 (7-8, 9-10)
Shown in size Medium

YARN
Rowan Wool Cotton (50% wool / 50% cotton; 123 yards / 50 grams): 5 (5, 6) skeins #956 coffee rich (dark brown; MC); 1 skein each #960 laurel (bright green; A), #955 ship shape (blue; B), #911 rich (red; C) and #942 mellow yellow (light yellow; D)

NEEDLES
One set of 5 double-pointed needles (dpn) size US 3 (3.25 mm)

Change needle size if necessary to obtain correct gauge.

NOTIONS
Stitch markers; yarn needle

GAUGE
24 sts and 33 rows = 4" (10 cm) in Stockinette stitch (St st)

NOTES
Socks are knit on four needles. The fifth needle is used to pick up gusset stitches.

CUFF
Using MC, CO 60 (64, 68) sts. Distribute sts on three needles as follows:
Needle one (N1) [half of back of sock]: 15 (16, 17) sts.

Needle two (N2) [top of sock]: 30 (32, 34) sts.
Needle three (N3) [half of back of sock]: 15 (16, 17) sts.

Join for working in the rnd, being careful not to twist sts; place marker for beginning of rnd. Begin k2, p2 rib; work even until piece measures 4" from beginning. Change to k1, p1 rib; work even until piece measures 6 ½" from beginning.

CALF AND BODY
Change to St st; work even until piece measures 9 ½" from beginning.

Shape Calf:
Next rnd, Decrease rnd: Work 1 st, ssk, work around to last 3 sts, k2tog, work 1 st.

Work 1 rnd even.
Change to A, work 2 rnds even.
Change to MC, work 1 rnd even.

Next rnd, Decrease rnd: Work 1 st, ssk, work around to last 3 sts, k2tog, work 1 st.

Work 1 rnd even.
Change to B, work 2 rnds even.
Change to MC, work 1 rnd even.

Next rnd, Decrease rnd: Work 1 st, ssk, work around to last 3 sts, k2tog, work 1 st.

Work 1 rnd even.
Change to C, work 2 rnds even.
Change to MC, work 1 rnd even.

Next rnd, Decrease rnd: Work 1 st, ssk, work around to last 3 sts, k2tog, work 1 st.

Work 1 rnd even.
Change to D, work 2 rnds even.
Change to MC and repeat Decrease rnd

every 5 rnds, 5 more times – 42 (46, 50) sts remain. Redistribute sts on needles as follows: 10 (11, 12) sts on N1, 22 (24, 26) sts on N2, and 10 (11, 12) sts on N3.

Work 38 rnds even.

HEEL FLAP
Next rnd: Using N3, work sts from N1 (all sts are now on two needles – 20 (22, 24) sts on N3 [heel] and 22 (24, 26) sts on N2 [front]).

Work back and forth on N3 [heel] as follows:
Row 1: (WS) Sl 1 st purlwise, purl to end.
Row 2: (RS) Sl 1 st knitwise, knit to end.

Repeat rows 1 and 2 for Heel Flap, 9 (10, 11) more times [20 (22, 24) heel rows].

TURN HEEL
Row 1: (RS) Sl 1 st knitwise, k11 (12, 13) sts, k2tog, k 1, turn, leaving remaining sts on left-hand needle.
Row 2: (WS) Sl 1 st purlwise, p5, p2tog, p1, turn, leaving remaining sts on left-hand needle.
Row 3: Sl 1 st knitwise, k6, k2tog, k1, turn.
Row 4: Sl 1 st purlwise, p7, p2tog, p1, turn.
Row 5: Sl 1 st knitwise, k8, k2tog, k1, turn.
Row 6: Sl 1 st purlwise, p9, p2tog, p1, turn.
Row 7: Sl 1 st knitwise, k10, k2tog, k1, turn.
Row 8 (size S only): Sl 1 st purlwise, p10, p2tog.
Row 8 (sizes M and L only): Sl 1 st purlwise, p11, p2tog, p1, turn – 12 (14, 16) sts remain on N3.

GUSSET
Resume working in the round. Work 6 (7, 8) sts from N3 on spare needle, then work remaining 6 (7, 8) sts on N1 (sts are again distributed on three needles).

Using N1 pick up and knit 12 (13, 14) sts along left side of heel flap; work 22 (24, 26) sts from N2; using N3, pick up and knit 12 (13, 14) sts along right side of heel flap; work remaining 6 (7, 8) sts from spare needle on N3 – 58 (64, 70) sts remain [18 (20, 22) sts on N1, 22 (24, 26) sts on N2, and 18 (20, 22) sts on N3].

Place marker for beg of rnd at center back of heel.

Rnd 1: Knit.
Rnd 2: Using N1, work to last 3 sts, k2tog, work 1 st; using N2, work to end; using N3, work 1 st, ssk, work to end.

Repeat Rnds 1 and 2 for Gusset, 7 (8, 9) more times – 42 (46, 50) sts remain [10 (11,12) sts on N1; 22 (24, 26) sts on N2, and 10 (11, 12) sts on N3]. Mark this rnd.

FOOT
Work even until foot measures 6 1/2 (7, 7 1/2)" from marker.

TOE
Shape Toe:
Rnd 1: Using N1, work to end; using N2, work 1 st, ssk, work to last 3 sts, k2tog, work 1 st; using N3, work to end – 40 (44, 48) sts remain.
Rnd 2: Knit.
Rnd 3: Using N1, work to last 3 sts, k2tog, work 1 st; using N2, work 1 st, ssk, work to last 3 sts, k2tog, work 1 st; using N3, work 1 st, ssk, work to end.

Repeat Rnds 2 and 3 for Toe Shaping, 4 (4, 5) more times – 20 (24, 24) sts remain.

Repeat Rnd 3 only, 2 (3, 3) times – 12 sts remain. Distribute sts on two needles [6 sts on each needle]. Break off yarn leaving a 16" tail. Thread tail onto yarn needle and graft sts together using Kitchener Stitch (see Special Techniques, page 137). Using yarn needle, weave in all loose ends.

I find that many of our best times at the store are when we are sitting with each other knitting, laughing, listening to music, and EATING something really yummy!

julie's
ORANGE HONEY MUFFINS

This recipe comes from Julie Stark. *She is an avid knitter who often bakes for us, consoles us, and at time even reads out loud to us at Group Therapy. Basically, she spoils us!*

For an extra-special treat, put a ¼-inch slice peeled, seeded orange in the bottom of each muffin cup before spooning in the batter.

MUFFINS
2   cups all-purpose flour
½   cup uncooked oatmeal, not instant
1   teaspoon baking powder
½   teaspoon salt
1   cup brown sugar
2   large eggs, slightly beaten
⅔   cup orange juice
Zest of 1 large orange
¼   cup honey
5½ tablespoons butter, melted

ICING
1-1½ cups powdered sugar
Approximately 1 tablespoon
    orange juice

Preheat oven to 350°F. Grease a twelve-cup muffin pan very well or line it with muffin papers.

Combine flour, oatmeal, baking powder, salt, and brown sugar in a large mixing bowl and stir with a wire whisk or a fork. Add the eggs, orange juice, orange zest, honey, and melted butter, and stir until just mixed. Spoon the batter into the muffin cups, filling each cup at least ⅔ full. Bake 20-25 minutes or until very light golden.

To make icing, combine powdered sugar with orange juice until a smooth glaze is formed. Drizzle over warm muffins. Muffins are best eaten warm, maybe while you contemplate your next row!

Makes twelve muffins.

CHANEL-ISH CARDIGAN JACKET
MARY-HEATHER COGAR

In the early twentieth century Coco Chanel created a look for women that was casual, comfortable, and liberating, a huge contrast to the corseted fashions of the time. Her style was particularly popular in free and easy California where movie stars embraced it right away. Chanel introduced her signature boxy cardigan-jacket in 1925 and it has never gone out of fashion. Women of all ages come into Knit Cafe requesting a pattern for a "Chanel-like jacket," so here it is. It is simple yet perfect for tea with the ladies or over jeans for shopping with the girls!

SIZES
Small (Medium, Large)
To fit women's bust size
32 (36, 40)"
Shown in size Small

FINISHED MEASUREMENTS
38 (41, 47¾)"

YARN
Filatura di Crosa Zara Plus
(100% extrafine merino
wool; 77 yards / 50 grams):
7 (9, 10) balls #28 dark gray
(MC) and 6 (7, 8) balls #27
light gray (CC)

NEEDLES
One pair straight needles
size US 7 (4.5 mm)

One 36" circular (circ)
needle size US 7 (4.5 mm)

Change needle size if
necessary to obtain
correct gauge.

NOTIONS
Stitch holders, stitch
markers, yarn needle, size
US E/4 (3.5 mm) crochet
hook for edging

GAUGE
18 sts and 30 rows = 4"
(10 cm) in Honeycomb Tweed
pattern (after blocking)

NOTES
The gauge of the Honeycomb Tweed
stitch pattern changes drastically when
blocked. It is essential to fully block
your swatches and match both stitch
and row gauge properly to ensure a
well-fitting jacket.

HONEYCOMB TWEED PATTERN
(worked over an odd number of sts)

Using MC CO.

Row 1 (RS): Change to CC, k1, *slip
1 st wyib, k1; repeat from * across.
Row 2: Purl.
Row 3: Change to MC, k2, *slip 1 st
wyib, k1; repeat from * across to
last st, k1.
Row 4: Purl.

Repeat Rows 1–4 rows for Honeycomb
Tweed pattern.

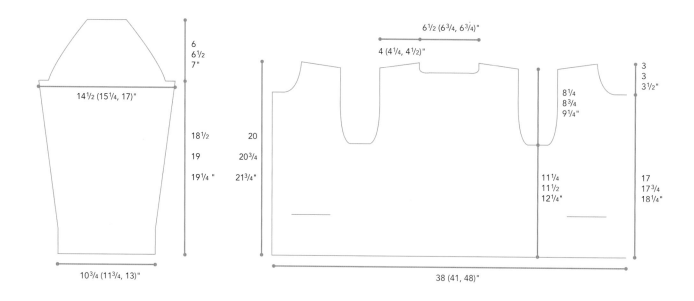

POCKET FLAP (make two)

Using MC and straight needles, CO 15 sts; begin Honeycomb Tweed pattern. Work 3 rows even, end with a RS row.

Shape Pocket Flap: (WS) Increase 1 st at each side on this row – 17 sts. Work as established until piece measures 1½" from beginning; place sts on holder.

BODY

Using MC and circ needle, CO 42 (46, 54) sts [Right Front], place marker (pm), 87 (93, 107) sts [Back], pm, 42 (46, 54) sts [Left Front] – 171 (185, 215) sts; beg Honeycomb Tweed pattern. Work 28 (32, 36) rows even, end with a WS row.

Pocket: (RS) Work 9 (11, 13) sts; *using MC, purl 17 sts [turning ridge]. Turn; purl 17 sts. Change to St st; work 37 rows even, end with a RS row. Keep Pocket sts on right needle.*

Rejoin CC to left side of this Pocket; work 119 (129, 155) sts [16 (18, 24) sts past second marker] in Honeycomb Tweed pattern. Repeat Pocket instructions from * to *. Rejoin CC yarn to left side of second Pocket; work in Honeycomb Tweed pattern to end.

Insert Pocket Flap: (WS) Work 9 (11, 13) sts as established; *With WS of Pocket Flap in front of WS of Garment, p2tog (1 st of Pocket Flap together with 1 st of Pocket)*; rep from * to * across until all Pocket Flap and Pocket sts have been worked; work across to second Pocket; repeat from * to * until all Pocket Flap and Pocket sts have been worked; work to end.

Work even in Honeycomb Tweed pattern until piece measures 11¼ (11½, 12¼)" from beginning, end with a WS row.

Divide for Fronts and Backs:

(RS) Work 38 (42, 48) sts and place on holder for Right Front, BO 8 (8, 12) sts, work 79 (85, 95) sts and place on holder for Back, BO 8 (8, 12) sts, work 38 (42, 48) sts for Left Front.

LEFT FRONT

With WS facing, purl 1 row.

Shape Armhole: (RS) Decrease 1 st at Armhole edge on this row, then every other row 6 (7, 10) times – 31 (34, 37) sts remain. Work even until Armhole measures 5¼ (5¾, 6)" from beg of shaping, end with a RS row.

Shape Neck: (WS) BO 8 (8, 10) sts at beginning of this row, then at neck edge, decrease 1 st every row 5 (7, 6) times – 18 (19, 21) sts remain. Work even until Armhole measures 8¼, 8¾, 9¼)" from beginning of shaping, end with a WS row.

Shape Shoulder: (RS) At Armhole edge, BO 6 (6, 7) sts twice, then 6 (7, 7) sts once.

RIGHT FRONT
Place sts on holder for Right Front on needle. With WS facing, join yarn at Armhole edge; work as for Left Front, reversing all shaping.

BACK
With WS facing, join yarn; purl 1 row.

Shape Armhole: (RS) Decrease 1 st at each side on this row then every other row 6 (7, 10) times – 65 (69, 73) sts remain.

Work even until Armhole measures 8 (8¼, 9)" from beginning of shaping, end with a WS row.

Shape Neck: (RS) Work 20 (21, 23) sts; join second ball of yarn and BO 25 (27, 27) sts; work to end.

Working both sides at the same time, at each neck edge, decrease 1 st every row twice, AND AT THE SAME TIME, when Armhole measures 8¼ (8¾, 9¼)" from beginning of shaping, end with a WS row and Shape Shoulders as for Fronts.

SLEEVES (make two)
Using MC and straight needles, CO 49 (53, 59) sts; begin Honeycomb Tweed pattern. Work 14 rows, end with a WS row.

Shape Sleeve: (RS) Increase 1 st at each side this row, then every 15 rows 6 (2, 4) times, every 16 rows 1 (5, 4) time(s), working increased sts in pattern as they become available – 65 (69, 77) sts. Work even until piece measures 18½ (19, 19¼)" from beginning, end with a WS row.

Shape Cap: BO 4 (4, 5) sts at beginning of next 2 rows, then at each side decrease 1 st every other row 7 (8, 10) times, every 3 rows 6 (6, 4) times, every other row 6 (7, 9) times – 19 (19, 21) sts remain. BO remaining sts.

FINISHING
Block pieces to measurements.

Sew shoulder seams. Set in Sleeves; sew Sleeve and side seams.

Crochet Edging: With RS facing, using MC and crochet hook, begin at lower edge of Left Front, work 1 round of single crochet across lower edge of garment, up Right Front, around neck edge, down Left Front; join with slip stitch to beginning of single crochet round. Join CC and work 1 round of Crab Stitch, alternating colors in each stitch by working 1 st MC and 1 st CC. Fasten off. With RS facing, using MC and crochet hook, work 1 round of single crochet around lower edge of Sleeves, beginning at seam; join with slip stitch to beginning of round. Join CC and work 1 round of Crab Stitch alternating colors in each st by working 1 st MC and 1 st CC. Fasten off.

With RS facing, using MC and crochet hook, work 1 row single crochet around edge of Pocket Flap.

Sew Pocket side edges together. Using yarn needle, weave in all loose ends. Lightly block Crochet Edging.

CLASSIC SWEATER FOR GUYS

Like my grandmother's classic chocolate cake, some recipes stand the test of time and need little, if any, fussing. The same philosophy holds true for this basic, straight, hip-length crewneck sweater, which most of the men who visit Knit Cafe prefer to busier styles. The neck is a little wider than you might expect; that's to show off the all-important T-shirt underneath. The yarn is the softest chunky baby alpaca I could find. The model is Todd, who actually prefers crocheting to knitting. He and his daughter Shelby bring a lot of joy to us at Knit Cafe.

SIZES
Small (Medium, Large, X-Large)

To Fit Men's Chest Sizes:
38 (40, 44, 48)".
Shown in size Small

FINISHED MEASUREMENTS
42 (44½, 48½, 52½)"

YARN
Misti Alpaca Chunky (100% baby alpaca; 108 yards / 50 grams): 10 (11, 12, 14) hanks #100 ecru

NEEDLES
One pair straight needles size US 11 (8 mm)

One 16" circular (circ) needle size US 11 (8 mm), for collar (optional)

Change needle size if necessary to obtain correct gauge.

NOTIONS
Stitch holders, yarn needle.

GAUGE
12 sts and 14 rows = 4" (10 cm) in Stockinette stitch (St st)

BACK
CO 63 (67, 73, 79) sts; begin in St st with a knit row. Work even until piece measures 12½ (13, 13¾, 14½)" from beginning, end with a WS row.

Shape Armholes: (RS) BO 3 (3, 3, 4) sts at beginning of next 2 rows, then at each side decrease 1 st every other row 2 (3, 5, 5) times – 53 (55, 57, 61) sts remain.

Work even until Armhole measures 9" (9¾, 9¾, 10¼)" from beginning of shaping, end with a WS row.

Shape Shoulders: (RS) BO 8 (8, 8, 9) sts at beginning of next 2 rows, 8 (9, 9, 9) sts at beginning of next 2 rows – 21 (21, 23, 25) sts remain. Place remaining sts on a holder for neck.

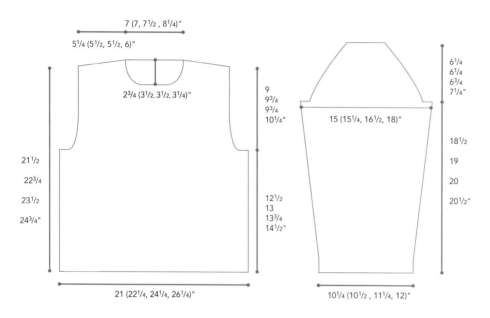

FRONT

Work as for Back until Armhole measures 6¼ (6¼, 6¼, 7)" from beginning of shaping, end with a WS row.

Shape Neck: (RS) Work 21 (22, 23, 24) sts; join second ball of yarn, work center 11 (11, 11, 13) sts and place on holder for neck, work to end. Working both sides at the same time, at each neck edge, decrease 1 st every row 5 (5, 6, 6) times – 16 (17, 17, 18) sts remain.

Work even until Armhole measures 9 (9¾, 9¾, 10¼)" from beginning of shaping, end with a WS row.

Shape Shoulders as for Back.

SLEEVES (make two)

CO 31 (32, 34, 36) sts; begin St st with a knit row. Work even until piece measures 2¼" from beginning, end with a WS row.

Shape Sleeve: (RS) Increase 1 st at each side on this row, then every 8 (8, 8, 6) rows 4 (4, 2, 2) times, every 9 (9, 8, 8) rows 2 (2, 5, 6) times – 45 (46, 50, 54) sts.

Work even until piece measures 18½ (19, 20, 20½)" from beginning, end with a WS row.

Shape Cap: BO 3 (3, 3, 4) sts at beginning of next 2 rows, then at each side, decrease 1 st every row 3 (3, 4, 4) times, decrease 1 st every other row 7 (7, 7, 8) times, decrease 1 st at every row 3 (3, 4, 4) times – 13 (14, 14, 14) sts remain. BO remaining sts.

FINISHING

Sew left shoulder seam. Set in Sleeves; sew Sleeve and side seams.

Rolled Collar:

Note: If you prefer a seamless collar, sew right shoulder seam before beginning the collar and use circular needle to work collar in round.

With RS facing, begin at Back neck, work 21 (21, 23, 25) sts from holder for Back neck, pick up and knit 13 (14, 15, 16) sts along left Front neck edge, work 11 (11, 11, 13) sts from holder for Front neck, pick up and knit 13 (14, 15, 16) sts along right Front neck edge – 58 (60, 64, 70) sts.

Rolled Collar worked flat: Purl the first row, then continue in St st for 9 (9, 9, 11) more rows. Sew right shoulder seam and collar.

Rolled Collar worked in the round: Place marker for the beginning of round. Work 10 (10, 10, 12) rounds in St st.

Using yarn needle, weave in all loose ends.

gadgets ARE GOOD

I am a sucker for gadgets. *I love them all – pretty scissors, cool stitch markers, nifty row counters, any kind of little case with compartments to hold it all. Yes, there are thrifty and practical ways to mark your stitches, but I would much rather use something fanciful. I especially love markers that remind me what I have to do, i.e., inc or dec or ssk or k2tog or knit or purl (like the ones I made for this photo).*

KNIT CAFE
—
90069
★ ★ ★ ★

COMFY SOCKS *aka this one & that one*
ULLI SCHOBER SHIBUYA

For years, I thought it was just me.

I would enjoy working on the first sock but would have no desire to make the second one. I've recently learned there is a name for this condition—SSS, or Second Sock Syndrome. Apparently, many other knitters suffer from it, too. To avert that problem here, the colors of the top of the cuff and the heel and toe change from one sock to the next.

SIZES
Small (Medium, Large)
To fit US woman's shoe size 6-7 (7½-8, 9)
Shown in size Small

YARN
Blue Sky Alpaca and Silk (50% alpaca / 50% silk; 146 yards / 50 grams): 2 skeins #i16 spring (light green; A) GGH Soft Kid (70% super kid mohair / 25% nylon / 5% wool; 154 yards / 25 grams): 1 skein each #048 seafoam blue (B) and #054 olive green (C)

NEEDLES
One set of 5 double-pointed needles size US 4 (3.5 mm)

One set of 5 double pointed needles (dpn) size US 4 (3.5 mm)

Change needle size if necessary to obtain correct gauge.

NOTIONS
Stitch marker, yarn needle

GAUGE
26 sts and 34 rows = 4" (10 cm) in Stockinette stitch (St st) using one strand of yarn A

CUFF
Using two strands of B or C held together and larger needles, CO 48 (52, 56) sts. Distribute sts on four needles [12 (13, 14) sts per needle]. Join for working in the rnd, being careful not to twist sts; place marker for beginning of rnd.

Begin in k2, p2 rib; work 2 rnds.

Change to one strand of A, and work as established until piece measures 2" from beginning.

CALF
Change to St st; work even until piece measures 6½ (7, 8)" from beginning.

HEEL
Work 24 (26, 28) sts [needle one (N1) and needle two (N2)]. Using needle three (N3) and needle four (N4), work back and forth as follows:

Row 1: (RS) *Slip 1 st purlwise with yarn in back, k1: repeat from * across.
Row 2: (WS) *Slip 1 st purlwise with yarn in front, p1; repeat from * across.

Repeat Rows 1 and 2 for Heel 4 (4, 5) more times.

Change to one strand of B or C and one strand of A held together, and work rows 1 and 2 for Heel 7 (8, 8) times [24 (26, 28) Heel rows].

TURN HEEL (continue with one strand of B or C and one strand of A held together):

Row 1: (RS): K14 (15, 16) sts, ssk, k1, turn.
Row 2: (WS) Slip 1 st purlwise with yarn in front, p5, p2tog, p1, turn.
Row 3: Slip 1 st purlwise with yarn in front, knit to 1 st before gap, ssk [1 st from each side of gap], k1, turn.
Row 4: Slip 1 st purlwise with yarn in front, purl to 1 st before gap, p2tog [1 st from each side of gap], p1, turn.

Repeat Rows 3 and 4 until all Heel sts have been worked – 14 (16, 16) sts remain. Break off B or C.

HEEL GUSSET (worked with one strand of A):

Resume working in the rnd. Work 14 (16, 16) sts, pick up and knit 12 (13, 14) sts from left side of heel, work 24 (26, 28) sts from N1 and N2, pick up and knit 12 (13, 14) sts on right side of heel, work 7 (8, 8) sts across half of heel, place marker for beginning of rnd [center back of Heel] – 62 (68, 72) sts [19 (21, 22) sts on N1; 12 (12, 14) sts on N2, 12 (12, 14) sts on N3; 19 (21, 22) sts on N4].

Shape Gusset:
Rnd 1: Using N1, work to last 3 sts, k2tog, work 1 st; using N2, work to end; using N3, work to end; using N4:, work 1 st, ssk, work to end.
Rnd 2: Knit.

Repeat Rnds 1 and 2 for Gusset, 6 (7, 7) more times – 48 (52, 56) sts remain. Mark this round.

FOOT
Work even in St st until foot measures 1½ (2, 2)" less than desired foot length from marker.

TOE (worked with one strand of B or C and one strand of A)

Change to one strand of B or C and one strand of A held together.

Shape Toe: Rnd 1: Using N1, work to last 3 sts, k2tog, work 1 st; using N2, work 1 st, ssk, work to end; using N3, work to last 3 sts, k2tog, work 1 st; using N4, work 1 st, ssk, work to end.
Rnd 2: Knit.

Repeat Rnds 1 and 2 for Toe, 5 (6, 6) more times – 24 (24, 28) sts remain.

Repeat Rnd 1 only 4 (4, 5) times – 8 sts remain. Distribute sts on two needles [4 sts on each needle]. Cut yarn, leaving a 16" tail. Thread tail onto yarn needle and graft sts together using Kitchener Stitch (see Special Techniques, page 137). Using yarn needle, weave in all loose ends.

1 CABLE, LONG TAIL, PROVISIONAL, THUMB, CROCHET 2 ENGLAND 3 138 STITCHES 4 749 YARDS 5 YARN IN FELTABLE FIBER, SUCH AS WOOL, MOHAIR, OR ALPACA, DETERGENT, AGITATION 6 FRONT 7 HANDWASH 8 D 9 KNIT 1 ROUND, PURL 1 ROUND, REPEAT 10 12 SKEINS 11 A, B or C 12 TWIST THE STITCH

stump THE KNITTER

At the end of Thursday Night Group Therapy, *it has become tradition for me to ask a random, sometimes obscure knitting question. Whoever gets the correct answer first wins a small prize. No calculators or reference materials are allowed. Here are some of the questions. Answers appear at bottom left.*

1 Name five different cast-ons.

2 Where was Elizabeth Zimmermann born?

3 You are making a 24" x 72" rectangular shawl with a gauge of 5.75 sts per inch. Without using a calculator, how many stitches should you cast on for the narrow end?

4 How many yards is 685 meters?

5 What are three requirements for felting?

6 Does the cable needle go to the front or the back of the work if you want a left-slanting cable?

7 What does the hand-in-the-tub symbol on a yarn label mean?

8 What is the measurement for "enough yarn"?
A. CLOSET FULL
B. TRUNK FULL
C. GARAGE FULL
D. ALL OF THE ABOVE

9 How do you do garter stitch in the round?

10 Your pattern calls for 9 50-gram skeins merino wool with 110 yards per skein. You decide to use a different yarn with the same gauge but only 87 yards per skein. How many skeins of the new yarn do you need?

11 Name at least one likely difference between a sweater knit in worsted-weight wool and a sweater knit in worsted-weight alpaca.
A. DRAPE
B. WARMTH
C. WEIGHT
D. AMOUNT OF YARN NEEDED

12 What does knitting into the back loop do?

COMPUTER KEYBOARD COVER

This keyboard cover makes a great gift. You can knit it in school colors or company colors or favorite colors. Make it stripey, add a monogram, or embellish it, as I did, with a fun pompom trim from a fabric store. The pattern, as written, fits a standard keyboard. If you need to adjust the size, add or subtract stitches based on your gauge. If you prefer a straight rectangular cover, just eliminate the increases and decreases.

FINISHED MEASUREMENTS
17" long by 6" wide

YARN
Gedifra Modern Cotton Elite (50% cotton / 35% viscose /15% polyester; 137 yards / 50 grams): 2 balls #3222 orange

NEEDLES
One pair straight needles size US 6 (4 mm)

One 32" circular (circ) needle size US 6 (4 mm)

Change needle size if necessary to obtain correct gauge.

NOTIONS
Stitch marker; 1 yard thin elastic cord to match cover color; yarn needle; approximately 1¼ yards ¼" wide pompom trim to match cover color (optional; determine exact length according to size of your keyboard); needle and thread to sew on trim

GAUGE
21 sts and 28 rows = 4" (10 cm) in Stockinette stitch (St st)

COVER
With straight needles, CO 42 sts; begin in St st.

Work 38 rows even, end with a WS row.

Shape Sides: (RS) Increase 1 st at each side on this row, then every 8 rows 3 times – 50 sts. Work 8 rows even, end with a WS row. Decrease 1 st at each side on this row, then every 8 rows 3 times – 42 sts remain.

Work 38 rows even, end WS row.

Change to circ needle. (RS) Work 42 sts, pick up and knit 100 sts along right side edge, 42 sts across cast-on edge, 100 sts along left side edge, place marker for beginning of rnd – 284 sts. Work 14 rnds in k2, p2 rib; BO all sts loosely.

FINISHING
Using yarn needle, weave in all loose ends; weave elastic in and out along bind-off round, gathering elastic slightly. Fasten ends of elastic together securely. *Optional: Using needle and thread, attach pompom trim around edge as shown in photograph.*

FELTED SADDLE BLANKET

I got the idea for this blanket while watching my daughter, Lilly, take her riding lesson. Beautiful Noro Kureyon yarn, a hand-dyed self-striping wool from Japan, is worked in a classic chevron pattern and then felted. It is sturdy enough for the wear and tear of a big saddle and soft enough to protect the horse's back.

FINISHED MEASUREMENTS
Before Felting:
Approximately 37" wide by 48" long

After Felting:
Approximately 33" wide by 38" long

YARN
Noro Kureyon (100% wool; 110 yards / 50 grams): 14 skeins #95

NEEDLES
One 36" circular (circ) needle size US 10 (6 mm)

Change needle size if necessary to obtain correct gauge.

NOTIONS
Stitch markers, yarn needle

GAUGE
22 sts and 20 rows = 4" (10 cm) in Chevron pattern before felting

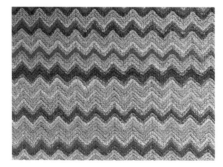

*CHEVRON PATTERN
(multiple of 12 sts + 3)
Row 1: K1, ssk, *place marker (pm), k9, slip 2 sts, k1, pass 2 slipped sts over k1; repeat from * across to last 12 sts, k9, k2tog, k1.
Row 2: K1, *p1, k4, [k1, yo, k1] in next st, k4; rep from * across to last 2 sts, p1, k1.
Repeat Rows 1 and 2 for Chevron pattern.

SADDLE BLANKET
CO 219 sts; knit 1 row. Change to Chevron pattern; work even until piece measures 48" from beginning, end with a WS row. BO all sts loosely. Using yarn needle, weave in all loose ends.

FELTING
Place Blanket in zippered pillowcase. Place pillowcase in washing machine and add small amount of detergent. Set machine for the smallest load size, hot wash, and cold rinse. Check felting progress every 1-2 minutes, depending on your machine, detergent, and local water conditions. When Blanket has felted to your liking, remove from washing machine and gently rinse in sink using tepid water. Roll blanket in several towels and squeeze out excess water. Place Blanket on a flat surface to dry.

FLUFFIEST BABY BLANKET

Super-soft and fluffy Trendsetter Zucca and GGH Esprit are two of the most popular yarns we sell at Knit Cafe, in part because of this easy, easy baby blanket, which many people are drawn to. It also makes a wonderful "big people" blanket. I made one twice as large for my home, and my kids and their friends rarely watch television without it. The two blankets shown here were knitted by Helene Roux, who always uses her wonderful French aesthetic to put together fun color combinations.

FINISHED MEASUREMENTS
Approximately 28" wide by 33" long

YARN
Trendsetter Zucca (58% tactel nylon / 42% polyamid; 72 yards / 50 grams): 5 balls #5570 purple OR GGH

Esprit (100% polyamid; 119 yards / 50 grams): 4 balls #33 pink, for Blanket body

Gedifra Techno Hair (100% polyamid; 98 yards / 50 grams): 1 ball #9607 apple green, for Blanket edging

NEEDLES
For Trendsetter Zucca: One pair straight needles size US 11 (8 mm)

For GGH Esprit: One pair straight needles size US 10.5 (6.5 mm)

NOTIONS
Size US J-10 (6 mm) crochet hook (for edging), yarn needle

GAUGE
For Trendsetter Zucca: 11 sts and 12 rows = 4" (10 cm) in Stockinette st (St st)

For GGH Esprit: 11 sts and 16 rows = 4" (10 cm) in St st

Note: Getting the exact gauge given is not important for this blanket.

BLANKET
Using Trendsetter Zucca or GGH Esprit, CO 77 sts; begin in St st. Work even until all yarn is used. BO all sts loosely.

FINISHING
Edging: Using crochet hook and Gedifra Techno Hair, work 1 rnd single crochet around edge of blanket; slip st to first single crochet. Fasten off. Using yarn needle, weave in all loose ends.

GUITAR MESSENGER BAG
BETH ABARAVICH

Beth is a fashion designer in Los Angeles who also works part-time at Knit Cafe. I love all of the details she worked into this messenger bag, especially the pocket on the back, the belt sliders for the adjustable strap, the sturdy denim lining inside, and the grosgrain ribbon lining the underside of the straps. I also adore the whimsy of her guitar motif but, obviously, it can be worked without it. The bag is knit in denim yarn, which WILL shrink. Note the gauge change before and after washing.

FINISHED MEASUREMENTS
Approximately 13" wide by 9" tall by 4½" deep (after washing)

YARN
Rowan Denim (100% cotton; 102 yards / 50 grams): 9 balls #225 Nashville (MC; dark blue); 1 ball #231 Tennessee (CC; light blue)

NEEDLES
One pair straight needles size US 5 (3.75 mm)

Change needle size if necessary to obtain correct gauge.

NOTIONS
Row markers; yarn needle; 2 belt sliders 1½" wide x 1" tall; 2 yards 1½" wide grosgrain or tapestry ribbon (for strap lining); ½ yard 60" wide heavy denim fabric for bag lining (optional)

GAUGE
Before washing: 20 sts and 30 rows = 4" (10 cm) in Stockinette stitch (St st)

After washing: 20 sts and 32 rows = 4" (10 cm) in Stockinette stitch (St st)

FLAP LINING, FLAP, AND BACK
Using MC, CO 65 sts; begin Garter st. Work 9 rows even, end with a RS row.

Next Row (WS): K6, work in St st (purl) to last 6 sts, k6. Continue as established, keeping first and last 6 sts of each row in Garter st and center 53 sts in St st, until piece measures 16¼" from beginning, end with a RS row. Knit 1 (WS) row [turning row]. Change to Garter st; work even for 8 rows, end with a WS row. Change to St st, keeping first and last 6 sts of each row in Garter st; work even for 2 rows, end with a WS row.

Establish Chart: Continuing with Garter st edging as established, work center 53 sts from Chart. Work even until Chart is complete. Continue in St st with Garter st edging until piece measures 16½" from end of Chart, end with a WS row. BO all sts.

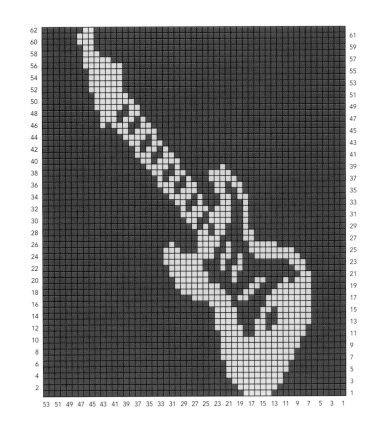

KEY

☐ St st – knit on RS,
   purl on WS

■ MC

☐ CC

FRONT
Using MC, CO 65 sts.

Next Row (RS): K6, work in St st
to last 6 sts, k6. Keeping first and
last 6 sts of each row in Garter st
and center 53 sts in St st, work even
until piece measures 12¾" from
beginning, end with a WS row.

Next Row (RS): Change to Garter
st and work even for 8 rows. BO all
sts knitwise.

BACK POCKET
Work as for Front until piece measures
8¾" from beginning, end with a WS row.

Next Row (RS): Change to Garter st
and work even for 8 rows. BO all
sts knitwise.

BOTTOM
Using MC, CO 65 sts; begin Garter
st. Work even until piece measures
7¾" from beginning, end with a
WS row. BO all sts knitwise.

LEFT SIDE
Using MC, CO 26 sts; begin Garter
st. *Work even until piece measures
3¼" from beginning, end with a
WS row.

Shape Sides: (RS) Decrease 1 st
each side on this row – 24 sts remain.
Repeat from * twice – 20 sts remain.
Work even until piece measures
13½" from beginning, end with a
WS row. Place row marker (pm)
at beginning and end of row for
finishing.

Shape Sides
Shape Sides: (RS) Decrease 1 st each
side every row 5 times – 10 sts remain.
Work even until piece measures 3"
from row marker. BO all sts knitwise.

RIGHT SIDE AND STRAP
Work as for Left Side until 10 sts
remain.

Strap: Work even until Strap measures
42". BO all sts knitwise.

FINISHING
Fold Flap Lining at turning row and
stitch to WS of Flap, so piece lies flat.
Sew sides of Flap. Sew Back Pocket
to Back of Bag (see schematic). Sew
CO/BO edge of Bottom to CO edge
of each Side. Sew Front to Bottom and
Sides, ending at row markers on Sides
and keeping long Strap on right side.

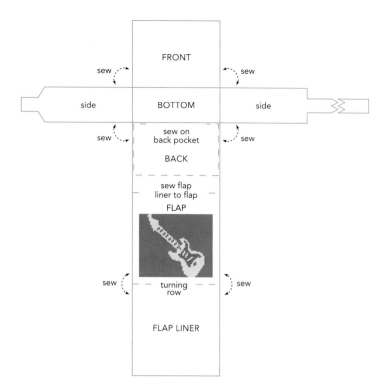

FRONT

sew ⟵ ⟶ sew

side | BOTTOM | side

sew ⟵ ⟶ sew

sew on
back pocket

BACK

sew flap
liner to flap

FLAP

sew ⟵ turning row ⟶ sew

FLAP LINER

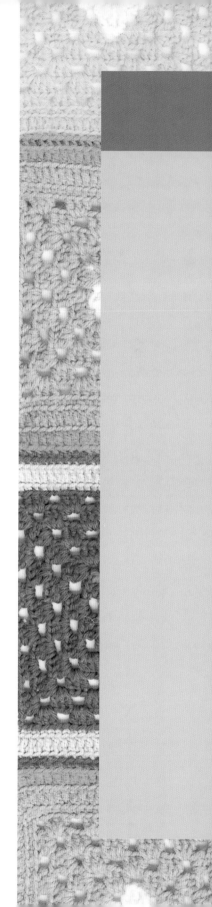

Sew Back to Bottom and Sides, matching row markers on Sides to seam at top of Flap. Remove markers; weave in all ends.

Washing: Place Bag in washing machine with small amount of laundry detergent and hot water. Wash on setting that will agitate Bag thoroughly. Put in clothes dryer and tumble dry completely.

Sew ribbon to inside of long Strap to prevent stretching. Slip short tab on left Side of Bag through one belt slider, avoiding floating bar of slider; fold tab in half to inside and stitch to itself. With RS of long Strap facing, slip Strap into slider from below, over floating bar and back down through slider, so that bar is not visible from RS of Strap (do not tighten Strap over bar). Slip

Strap through slider on left Side of Bag, avoiding bar; fold Strap back on itself so linings are facing in, slip end of Strap back into slider (underneath other end of long Strap), over bar, then through slider; fold end over 1" and stitch to itself.

Lining (optional): Determine finished measurements of Front, Sides, and Bottom of Bag (excluding Straps) and add ½" to all sides of pieces. Lay out lining material and cut 2 front pieces, 2 side pieces, and one bottom piece. Using ½" seam allowance, sew pieces together, leaving top edges unfinished. Fold top ½" of Lining to WS of fabric and press flat. Sew seam around entire top of Lining, ³⁄₈" from top. Place Lining in Bag and whipstitch to Bag just below inside top edge.

The criteria for a CD to make this list is simple. My customers and I must be able to listen to it at least three times in a row without anyone feeling like they want to get up to change it.

Music is a big part of my life *at home and in the store. I am almost never without it. I suspect that I am not alone in my passion and need for music to help me feel my many moods. The CD player at Knit Cafe runs just about 24/7 and in the past three years* we've gone through two new CD players and one IPOD!

KNIT CAFE'S
top 10 cd's

NORAH JONES FEELS LIKE HOME

INDIA ARIE ACOUSTIC SOUL

EARTH, WIND & FIRE GREATEST HITS

STEVE TYRELL A NEW STANDARD

PAUL SIMON 1964/1993

MILES DAVIS LOVE SONGS

CESARIA EVORA CAFÉ ATLANTICO

MADELINE PEYROUX CARELESS LOVE

THE BEST OF MARVIN GAYE – THE 70'S

KISSING JESSICA STEIN SOUNDTRACK

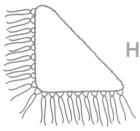

HUGE TRIANGLE SHAWL

This alpaca shawl won't be the quickest knit and it won't be the most riveting knit but it will definitely become one of your most treasured creations. I thought long and hard about adding some fancy stitchwork to the design—it's all Stockinette stitch—to make the process of making it more interesting, but frankly, when I buy or make an expensive shawl, I always like it luxurious and simple. That way, I know I'll get a lot of use out of it.

FINISHED MEASUREMENTS
Approx. 88" wide by 30" long (measured down center spine)

YARN
Blue Sky Alpacas (100% alpaca; 120 yards / 50 grams): 9 balls #005 natural taupe

NEEDLES
One 32" circular (circ) needle size US 6 (4mm)

One 40" circular (circ) needle size US 6 (4mm)

Change needle size if necessary to obtain correct gauge.

NOTIONS
Yarn needle, row counter, size E/4 (3.5 mm) crochet hook (for fringe)

GAUGE
19 sts and 28 rows = 4" (10 cm) in Stockinette st (St st)

NOTE
Work increases 3 sts in from each side. I like knitting into the front and back of the stitch (k-f/b), but a yarnover (yo) increase is also nice.

Beginning at lower edge of garment, using shorter circular needle, CO 2 sts.

Work 200 rows in St st, and at the same time, increase 1 st at each side on every row – 402 sts. Change to longer circ needle when necessary to accommodate sts.

Increase 2 sts at each side of next 4 rows – 418 sts.

BO stitches loosely.

FINISHING
Using yarn needle, weave in all loose ends. Block lightly.

Fringe: Cut four 16" lengths of yarn. Taking all 4 strands together and using crochet hook, attach fringe to shawl at top corner of one of the diagonal edges. (If you do not know how to make fringe, see page 137.) Continue to cut and attach fringe along both diagonal edges, spacing them about 1" apart. (You will be cutting approximately 380 16" strands to create approximately 95 4-strand fringes). Once all the fringe is attached, tie together half of the strands from each fringe to half the fringe on its right and left (see photo). Trim fringe evenly.

JUDY'S GRANDMOTHER'S BABY SWEATER

JUDY SPECTOR *or the best-fitting, no seam, reversible baby sweater*

Soon after I opened Knit Cafe, Judy showed me this adorable reversible sweater, which is based on a design passed down to her from her grandmother. I was drawn to its style as well as the way it's knitted—you work it from side to side, starting with 6 stitches for the strap. I immediately arranged with Judy to carry the pattern in the shop and since then I have seen it worked in cashmere, cashmerino, alpaca, merino wool, wool-cotton, and cotton.

SIZES
Newborn/Infant (6 Months)
Shown in size 6 months

FINISHED MEASUREMENTS
Chest: 16 (18)"
Shoulder to hem: 9 (10)"
Shoulder to cuff: 8 (9)"

YARN
Classic Elite Premiere
(50% cotton / 50% Tencel;
108 yards / 50 grams):
4 balls #5212 mimosa
(creamy, pale yellow)

NEEDLES
One pair straight needles
size US 5 (3.75 mm)

One set double-pointed
needles (dpn) size US 5
(3.75 mm)

Change needle size
if necessary to obtain
correct gauge.

NOTIONS
Point protectors, row
markers, yarn needle

GAUGE
23 sts and 40 rows = 4"
(10 cm) in Garter stitch

It looks great in all of them, but my personal favorite is Classic Elite's Premiere Pima Cotton with Tencel, which is a baby-soft, luxurious yarn that comes in really pretty colors and is environmentally friendly (Tencel—the trade name for the generic fiber lyocell—is a completely biodegradable fiber made from the wood pulp from trees grown on managed farms.) Once, while on a trip to New York, I made this sweater, then ripped it out and made it again, not because there was anything wrong with my work but because I didn't have another project to work on and all the yarn shops in town were closed. I know that seems nutty to some people. All I can tell you is it's a really fun pattern and I enjoy it every time I work on it! In the photo at right Komari is wearing the "back" of the sweater in front.

NOTES

Piece is worked from side to side. Sleeves are picked up and worked shoulder to cuff.

All shaping (increases and decreases of one stitch only) is worked 2 stitches in from the edge.

Selvedge stitches are counted as part of the piece. For entire garment, on every row, knit first stitch through back side of loop (KB1), and slip last stitch with yarn in front.

STITCH GUIDE

Honeycomb Stitch (worked over an even number of sts)

Row 1 (RS): Knit.
Row 2: K1, *Slip 1 st, k1; repeat from * across to last st, k1.
Row 3: Knit.
Row 4: K2, *Slip 1 st, k1; repeat from * across.

Repeat Rows 1-4 for Honeycomb pattern.

BODY

Using Cable Cast On Method (see page 137), CO 6 sts; begin in Garter st. Work even until piece measures 13 (15)" from beginning (working Selvedge sts as indicated in Notes throughout).

Increase 1 st at beginning of every row (2 sts in from edge) 46 (60) times – 52 (66) sts, end with WS row. Mark this row.

Change to Honeycomb pattern; work even until piece measures 2½ (3)" from row marker, end with WS row.

Next row: (RS) Using dpn, work 19 (22) sts; place point protectors on the ends to use as holder; work to end as established – 33 (44) sts.

Next row: Work 33 (44) sts in pattern as established, then using the Backward Loop Cast On method (see page 137), CO 19 (22) sts above sts held on dpn [Armhole opening] – 52 (66) sts. Mark this row.

Work even as established until piece measures 2½ (3)" from row marker, end with WS row (Row 2 or 4).

Shape Neck: (RS) BO 4 (5) sts, work to end – 48 (61) sts remain. At neck edge, decrease 1 st on this row, then every row 3 (4) times – 44 (56) sts remain.

Work even as established for another 2 (2½)", end with RS row.

Shape Neck: At neck edge, increase 1 st [K1B (invisible increase)] on this row, then every row next 3 (4) times – 48 (61) sts.

Work 1 (0) row even in pattern.

Next row (RS): Using Backward Loop Cast On method, CO 4 (5) sts; work to end as established – 52 (66) sts.

Work even as established for another for 2 ½ (3)", end with WS row.

Next row: (RS) Using dpn, work 19 (22) sts; place point protectors on the ends to use as holder; work to end as established – 33 (44) sts.

Next row: Work 33 (44) sts in pattern as established, then using the Backward Loop Cast On method, CO 19 (22) sts above sts held on dpn [Armhole opening] – 52 (66) sts. Mark this row.

Work as established until piece measures 2½ (3)" from row marker, end with a WS row.

Change to Garter st, AND AT THE SAME TIME, decrease 1 st at the beginning of every row 8 (10) times – 44 (56) sts.

Shape Opening for Ties: (RS) Work 2 sts, k2tog, work 4 (6) sts, BO 28 (36) sts, work to end.

Next row: Work 2 sts, k2tog, work 4 (6) sts; turn work, and using the Cable Cast On Method, CO 28 (36) sts above the bound-off sts from previous row, work to end.

Continue to decrease 1 st at beginning of every row in this manner until 6 sts remain. Work even until piece measures 13 (15)" from last decrease row. BO all sts.

SLEEVES (make two)

Note: Sleeve is worked with seam edge (open edge) at shoulder and closed edge under the arm to make it smooth against baby's body.

Begin with Right Sleeve, remove one end protector from dpn at Armhole, and using same needle pick up and knit 19 (22) sts from bound-off edge – 38 (44) sts. Work in Honeycomb pattern until Sleeve measures 4½ (5)" from pick-up row, end with a WS row.

Cuff: Size Newborn/Infant only: (RS) K2, k2tog, [k6, k2tog] 4 times, k2 – 33 sts remain.

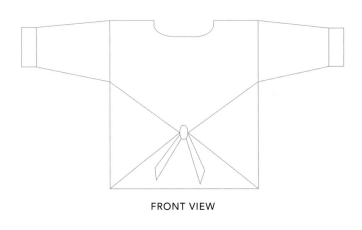

FRONT VIEW

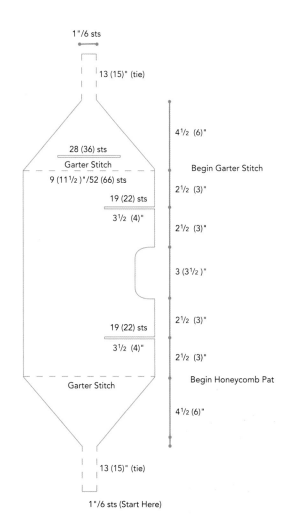

1"/6 sts

13 (15)" (tie)

4½ (6)"

28 (36) sts

Garter Stitch

9 (11½)"/52 (66) sts

Begin Garter Stitch

2½ (3)"

19 (22) sts

3½ (4)"

2½ (3)"

2½ (3)"

3 (3½)"

19 (22) sts

3½ (4)"

2½ (3)"

2½ (3)"

Garter Stitch

Begin Honeycomb Pat

4½ (6)"

13 (15)" (tie)

1"/6 sts (Start Here)

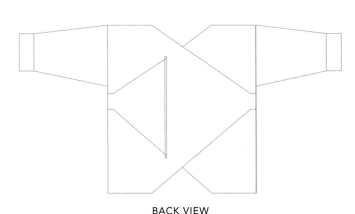

BACK VIEW

Size 6 months only: (RS) K2, k2tog, k6, (k2tog, k3) 6 times, k2tog, k2 – 36 sts remain.

Both Sizes: Work 8 rows even in Garter st, end with a RS row

Using Elastic Bind Off (see page 137), BO VERY LOOSELY, until 1 st remains. DO NOT CUT YARN.

FINISHING

Right Sleeve Seam: With WS facing, using dpn with point protector on one end, begin with remaining cuff stitch, pick up and knit 1 stitch in each selvedge loop along side edge of Sleeve from cuff to neck; place point protector at second end of this needle. Fold sleeve up and turn work. Using second dpn, with point protector on one end, and SAME yarn, continue to pick up and knit an equal number of sts along other side edge of Sleeve, begin at first row of Garter st to cuff. *Note: Needles are close and tight.*

Holding two needles together, work Three-Needle Bind Off (see page 138) to close sleeve/shoulder seam.

Left Sleeve Seam: With WS facing, using dpn with point protector on one end, begin with remaining cuff stitch, pick up and knit 1 stitch in each selvedge loop along side edge from cuff to last row of Garter st; place point protector at second end of this needle. Fold sleeve up and turn work. Using second dpn with point protector at one end and SAME yarn, continue to pick up and knit an equal number of sts along other side edge of Sleeve, neck edge to cuff.

Holding two needles together, work Three-Needle Bind Off to close sleeve/shoulder seam.

When 1 st remains, pick up and knit around curved part of front neck edge from left to right shoulder. Turn work and bind off all sts. Using yarn needle, weave in loose ends.

KAT'S PRETTY PINK DRESS
KAT COYLE

Our neighborhood bakery, Sweet Lady Jane,
is just a block from Knit Cafe. Jane, a longtime knitter, is legendary in Los Angeles for her frothy cakes, scrumptious scones, and English teas. The bakery seemed the perfect backdrop for Kat's concoction of delicate, soft pink mohair. I had asked Kat to design a short pink dress and, as I knew she would, she infused it with her special sense of femininity, fun, and flair. I love the delicateness of this dress, especially the neckline shaping and the touch of blue around the neckline and hem.

SIZES
Small (Medium, Large)
Shown in size Small

FINISHED MEASUREMENTS
30 (34, 38)" chest

YARN
Knit One, Crochet Too
Douceur et Soie (70% mohair / 30% silk;

225 yards / 25 grams):
4 (4, 5) skeins #8243 ballerina pink (MC)

GGH Soft Kid (70% super kid mohair / 25% nylon / 5% wool; 151 yards / 25 grams): approximately 4 yards #058 hazy teal (CC) for embroidery on hem and neckline

NEEDLES
One 24" circular (circ) needle size US 5 (3.75 mm)

One pair straight needles size US 7 (4.5 mm)

Change needle size if necessary to obtain correct gauge.

NOTIONS
Crochet hook size D/3 (3.25 mm)

Stitch markers, yarn needle

GAUGE
18 sts and 30 rows = 4" (10 cm) in Eyelet Pattern using smaller needles and MC

NOTES
Front and Back are worked back and forth on circ needles.

Decrease Row: (RS) Work 1 st, ssk, work across to last 3 sts, k2tog, work 1 st.

When working decreases on the Front and Back, if there are insufficient sts to work a complete repeat of the pattern after working the decrease at the right edge or before working the decrease at the left edge, work the remaining pattern sts in St st. Do not work a yo in the Eyelet Pattern without a corresponding decrease.

When working increases on the Front and Back, work increased sts in St st until you have sufficient sts to work an entire repeat of the Eyelet Pattern.

PATTERN STITCHES
Eyelet Pattern
(multiple of 8 sts; 16-row repeat)

Row 1 (WS) and all WS rows: Purl.
Row 2: Knit.
Row 4: K3, *yo, ssk, k6; repeat from * across to last 5 sts, yo, ssk, k3.
Row 6: K1, *k2tog, yo, k1, yo, ssk, k3; repeat from * across to last 7 sts, k2tog, yo, k1, yo, ssk, k2.

Row 8: K2, *k2tog, yo, k6; repeat from * across to last 6 sts, k2tog, yo, k4.

Row 10: Knit.

Row 12: K7, *yo, ssk, k6; repeat from * across to last st, k1.

Row 14: K5, *k2tog, yo, k1, yo, ssk, k3; repeat from * across to last 3 sts, k3.

Row 16: K6, *k2tog, yo, k6; repeat from * across to last 2 sts, k2.

Repeat Rows 1–16 for Eyelet pattern.

Front and Back (both alike)
Using MC and circ needle, CO 88 (96, 104) sts.

Establish Pattern

Row 1 (WS): P12, place marker (pm), work in Eyelet Pattern across center 64 (72, 80) sts, pm, p12.

Row 2: K12, slip marker (sm), work in Eyelet Pattern to next marker, sm, k12.

Continue in pattern as established until you have completed Row 13 of Eyelet Pattern.

Shape Body: *Note: Remove markers when they are within 3 sts of either edge.* Work Decrease Row every 14 rows 6 times, then every 6 rows 8 times – 60 (68, 76) sts remain. Work even for 1¾", end on a WS row.

(RS) Increase 1 st each side every 16 rows 4 times, as follows: K1, m1, work to last st, m1, k1 – 68 (76, 84) sts. Work even for 5 rows, ending on a WS row.

Shape Armholes and Neck: (RS) Decrease 4 sts evenly across row as follows:

Sizes S and L: Work 1 st, ssk, work 28 (36) sts, k2tog, work 2 sts, ssk, work 28 (36) sts, k2tog, work 1 st – 64 (80) sts remain.

Size M: Work 1 st, ssk, work 32 sts, k2tog, work 2 sts, ssk, work 32 sts, k2tog, work 1 st – 72 sts remain.

All sizes: Purl 1 (WS) row.

Next Row, Decrease Row: (RS) Work 1 st, ssk, work 26 (30, 34) sts, k2tog, work 1 st; join a second ball of yarn; work 1 st, ssk, work to last 3 sts, k2tog, work 1 st – 30 (34, 38) sts remain each side. Working both sides at same time, purl 1 (WS) row. Repeat Decrease Row every other row 13 (15, 17) times – 4 sts remain.

RUFFLE
Using MC and larger needles, CO 6 sts.

Establish Pattern:

Row 1 (RS): K3, [yo] twice, k2tog, k1 – 7 sts.

Row 2: K3, p1, k3.

Rows 3, 4, and 7: Knit.

Row 5: K3, [yo] twice, k2tog, [yo] twice, k2 – 10 sts.

Row 6: K3, p1, k2, p1, k3.

Row 8: BO 4 sts (leaving 1 st on right-hand needle), k5 – 6 sts remain.

Repeat rows 1 – 8 until piece measures approximately 121 (133, 144)" from beginning, end with Row 8 of pattern. BO all sts.

FINISHING
Block pieces lightly. Sew side seams.
Neck Edging: Using crochet hook and MC, beginning at top of left Back neck edge, work 1 rnd sc around neck and armhole edges, join with a sl st to first sc; fasten off.

Straps (make 4): Using crochet hook and MC, join yarn with slip st at neckline point, work chain st until Strap measures 11" from beginning.

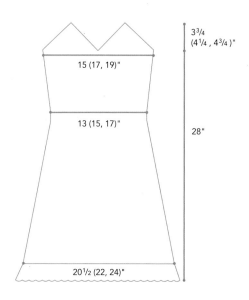

Turn and work 1 sc in each ch across, sl st to neckline point; fasten off. Tie Straps in bows at shoulders.

Ruffle: Using MC, baste a running stitch along straight edge of Ruffle, 1 st in from edge. Gather to fit along bottom edge of Dress. Pin Ruffle to RS of Dress, just above CO edge. Using MC and backstitch, sew Ruffle to Dress, 2 sts in from edge of Ruffle, allowing edge to ripple. Sew CO and BO edges of Ruffle together. Using yarn needle, weave in all loose ends.

Embroidery: Using yarn needle and CC, beginning and ending at center Front, embroider a running st along neck and armhole edges, just below single crochet edging. Tie ends in bow. Using yarn needle and 2 strands CC held together, begin and end at left side seam, embroider a running st in bottom edge of dress, above Ruffle. Tie ends in bow.

KIDS' CLUB FAVORITE SKIRT

This playful skirt is one of Knit Cafe's signature patterns. When I first introduced it, moms and grandmothers who saw it in the shop were eager to make it for the young girls in their lives. As time went on, I started getting calls from knitters all over the country, explaining that a little girl they knew had been coveting it ever since she'd spotted it on a friend. Not surprisingly, the kids in our Kids' Club were drawn to the skirt as well. Once we had decided to make it a Kids' Club project—and saw all the fun, crazy combinations the kids came up with—we decided to name the skirt

STANDARD CHILDREN'S HIP MEASUREMENTS
To ensure a good fit, it is always best to take the measurement of the child you are making the skirt for. If that isn't possible, refer to the chart below.

YARN
Yardage based on worsted-weight yarn with a gauge of approximately 4½–5 sts per inch

NEEDLES
Whatever size 32" or 36" long circular needle necessary to get an appropriate gauge with main yarn (knitted fabric should be smooth and drape nicely – it should not be too loose or tight)

NOTIONS
Stitch marker, yarn needle

	1 YEAR	2 YEARS	4 YEARS	6 YEARS	8 YEARS	10 YEARS	12 YEARS
HIP	21"	22"	24"	26"	28"	30"	32"
YARN	250 yards	300 yards	375 yards	400 yards	500 yards	550 yards	600 yards

after the club. It's a skirt with no rules and a wonderful way to use up stash yarn. The pattern is actually a worksheet with blanks to be filled in based on the size you are making and the gauge of your main yarn. This gives you a lot of freedom. I recommend that you choose a strong cotton or wool blend as the main yarn to provide structure. Then go wild adding stripes of zanier stuff like fluffy yarns and ribbon or eyelash yarns.

favorite skirt worksheet

STEP 1
Make a gauge swatch with your main yarn and check your stitches per inch.

[   ] **X** [   ] **=** [   ]

STEP 2
Measure hips (in inches).

STEP 3
Multiply the hip measurement by stitches per inch.

STEP 4
Round to the nearest multiple of 6.

[   ]

This is the number of stitches you will cast on.

START KNITTING SKIRT
Using MC and circular needle, cast on _____ sts.
Join for working in the rnd, being careful not to twist sts; place marker for beginning of rnd.

Rnds 1 to 3: *K3, p3; rep from * around.
Rnd 4 (Eyelet rnd): K4, *yo, k2tog; rep from * around.

Rnds 5 to 7: *K3, p3; rep from * around.

Work in St st (knit every rnd), adding colors and yarns as you wish. Remember to come back to the MC yarn often.

When your skirt is 1" shorter than you want it, work 1" in k3, p3 ribbing.

BO all sts loosely in ribbing. Using yarn needle, weave in all loose ends.

I-cord drawstring: Using dpn, CO 3 sts and knit 1 row. Slide the sts to the other end of the needle and knit, pulling yarn across the row. Repeat until the I-cord is approximately 10" longer than desired waist measurement. BO all sts. Thread I-cord through Eyelet rnd.

KNIT CAFE BASIC HAT

It seems like knitters are always looking for a basic hat pattern and every store has its own favorite to offer. This is the one we feature at Knit Cafe. It works perfectly as a plain well-fitting hat but is super-fun to make and wear when you come up with your own yarn, color, or stitch combinations. I'm partial to stripes and have many, many versions in my private stash. Personalize it any way you want—add a pompom, tassels, whatever.

SIZES
Baby (Child, Adult Small/
Medium, Adult Medium/
Large)

FINISHED MEASUREMENTS
14 (18, 20, 22)"

YARN
Approximately 125
(160, 200, 250) yards
worsted-weight yarn

NEEDLES
Appropriate size 16" circular
(circ) needle: approximately
US size 7 (4.5 mm) to 9
(5.5 mm)

Change needle size to
achieve desired gauge.

NOTIONS
Stitch marker, yarn needle

GAUGE
Approximately 4 to 5 sts = 1"

basic hat worksheet

STEP 1
Make a gauge swatch approximately 4" square. If you like the way the fabric feels, measure how many stitches are in an inch.

If you don't like the way the fabric feels, make another swatch with a different size needle (larger needles if your swatch feels too tight and smaller needles if your swatch feels too loose).

STEP 2
Multiply your stitches per inch by 14 for a Baby, 18 for a Child, 20 for an Adult Small/Medium, or 22 for an Adult Medium/Large.

STEP 3
Round this number to the nearest multiple of 8.

This is the number of stitches you will cast on.

BEGIN WORKING HAT

Cast on _____ stitches. Join for working in the rnd, being careful not to twist sts; place marker for beginning of rnd.

Work 4 rows k1, p1 ribbing for a ribbed-bottom hat, then switch to St st; OR work the entire hat in St st for a rolled-bottom hat. Continue working in St st (since you are working in the round, just knit every round) until your hat measures 4½ (5, 6½, 6½)" from the beginning.

SHAPE TOP OF HAT

Round 1: *K6, k2tog; repeat from * around.
Round 2: Knit.
Round 3: *K5, k2tog; repeat from * around.
Round 4: Knit.
Round 5: *K4, k2tog; repeat from * around.
Round 6: Knit.
Round 7: *K3, k2tog; repeat from * around.
Round 8: Knit.
Round 9: *K2, k2tog; repeat from * around.

Round 10: Knit.
Round 11: *K2tog; repeat from * around.

Cut yarn, leaving an 8" tail. Thread tail through remaining sts on needle and pull tight. Thread needle through to inside of hat, secure tail, and using yarn needle, weave in all loose ends. If you like, add a pompom or other embellishment.

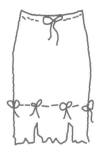

LACY SKIRT WITH BOWS
KAT COYLE

This contemporary skirt with a vintage flair is worked back and forth from the bottom up. The front and the back are the same. The bottom half is made of lace panels, three in the front and three in the back. It looks pretty with a delicate blouse but is just as much fun with a sweater and boots.

SIZES
Small (Medium, Large)

FINISHED MEASUREMENTS
(without drawstring)
Waist: 26 (30, 41½)"
Hips: 30 (37, 49)"
Length: 23"

Shown in size Small

YARN
Twisted Sisters Daktari Monochromatic Variegate (100% cotton, slubbed; 145 yards / 50 grams): 4 (5, 6) skeins #120166 cappuccino (tan; MC)

Lana Grossa India (100% nylon; 60 yards / 50 grams): 1 skein #03 tan (CC)

NEEDLES
Two 24" circular (circ) needles size US 6 (4 mm)

One 24" circ needle size US 5 (3.75 mm)

Change needle size if necessary to obtain correct gauge.

NOTIONS
Size G/6 (4 mm) crochet hook, yarn needle, row counter

GAUGE
21 sts and 29 rows = 4" (10 cm) in Stockinette stitch (St st) using smaller needles

25 sts = 4" (10 cm) in Lace Pattern using larger needles

NOTES
One of the larger circular needles is used to hold lace panels while others are being worked.

PATTERN STITCHES
Lace Pattern (multiple of 12 sts plus 1)

Rows 1–4: Knit.
Rows 5, 7, 9, and 11: (WS) K1, *k2tog twice, [yo, k1] 3 times, yo, ssk twice, k1; repeat from * across.
Rows 6, 8, 10, and 12: Purl.
Repeat Rows 1–12 for Lace pattern.

FRONT AND BACK
(make two, both alike)

Lace Panels: (make three, all alike)
Using MC and larger needles and the Long-Tail Cast On Method, CO 37 (49, 61) sts. Begin in Lace pattern; work 24 rows even, end with a WS row. Work first and second panels, cut yarn and place live sts on spare larger circular needle for later joining, then work third panel, do not cut yarn.

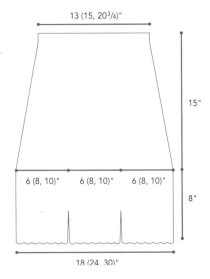

13 (15, 20¾)"

15"

6 (8, 10)" 6 (8, 10)" 6 (8, 10)"

8"

18 (24, 30)"

Joining Lace Panels: *Beginning with third panel, work 36 (48, 60) sts of Row 25 (Row 1 of third repeat of Lace pattern), k2tog (the last st of third panel with first st of second panel), work 35 (47, 59) sts, k2tog (the last st of second panel with the first st of first panel), work to end* – 109 (145, 181) sts [three panels are joined].

Work even in Lace pattern until Row 48 is complete.

Eyelet Band

Change to smaller needles.

Row 49: [K20 (27, 35), k2tog] 4 times, k21 (29, 33) – 105 (141, 177) sts remain.
Row 50: P1, k to last st, p1.
Row 51: [K19 (27, 24), k2tog, k20 (26, 23), k2tog] 2 (2, 3) times, k19 (27, 24) – 101 (137, 171) sts remain.
Row 52: Repeat Row 50.
Row 53: K1, *k2tog, yo twice; repeat from * across to last 2 sts, k2.
Row 54: P1, *knit all sts, working the first yo and dropping the second yo; repeat from * across to last st, p1.
Row 55: [K18 (26, 23), k2tog] 4 (4, 6) times, k21 (25, 21) – 97 (133, 165) sts remain.
Row 56: Repeat Row 50.

Body

Change to St st.

Sizes Small and Med only:
Row 57: [K9 (13), k2tog] 8 times, k9 (13) – 89 (125) sts remain.
Row 58 and all even-numbered rows: Purl.
Row 59: [K28 (12), k2tog] 2 (8) times, k29 (13) – 87 (117) sts remain.
Row 61: [K28 (22), k2tog] 2 (4) times, end k27 (21) – 85 (113) sts remain.

Size Large only:
Row 57: [K17, k2tog, k16, k2tog] 4 times, end k17 – 157 sts remain.

Row 58 and all even-numbered rows: Purl.
Row 59: [K16, k2tog, k15, k2tog] 4 times, k17 – 149 sts remain.
Row 61: [K20, k2tog, k19, k2tog] 3 times, k20 – 143 sts.

All Sizes:

Rows 62–66: Begin with a purl (WS) row, work even in St st.
Row 67: K1, ssk, k to last 3 sts, k2tog, k1 – 83 (111, 141) sts remain.

Work 11 (5, 5) rows even in St st. Repeat last 12 (6, 6) rows 7 (11, 11) times more – 69 (89, 119) sts remain.

Sizes Med and Large only: Decrease 1 st each end as above on next row. Work 3 rows even in St st. Repeat last 4 rows 4 times more – (79, 109) sts.

All Sizes: Work 5 (3, 3) rows even in St st.

WAISTBAND

Row 1: (WS) K1, p to last st, k1.
Row 2: P1, k to last st, p1.
Row 3: Knit.
Row 4: P2, * yo, p2tog; repeat from * across to last st, p1.
Row 5: Knit.
Row 6: Repeat Row 2.
Bind off all sts purlwise.

FINISHING

Begin at first row of lower eyelet Band, sew Front and Back pieces together. Using yarn needle, weave in loose ends. Handwash skirt; lay flat to dry. Block lightly. **Drawstring:** Using CC and crochet hook, work chain st until piece measures 40 (48, 56)" long from beginning; fasten off. Begin at center Front, weave Drawstring in and out of Waistband eyelets. Using CC, cut 12 strands yarn 20 (24, 28)" long. Using 2 strands yarn held together, weave through eyelets in Lower Band. Tie off in 6 bows, 1 at each side, 2 in Front, and two in Back, placed above slits.

BENEFITS OF lavender

I learned about them the painful way.
I'm writing about moths. I knew they were out there. I knew anyone could get them. But I didn't know that I could get them. I'll spare you my tragic details and bring you up to date with what I've learned.

Moths love natural, synthetic, and natural-blended fibers. Basically, that means everything. They are attracted to the human scents and smells that are on all of our fabrics and yarns. It is essential to regularly clean out, vacuum, and wash areas where fibers are stored. Lavender is a natural repellant to moths. Another way to protect your fibers from moths is to wash everything with a cleaning agent with lavender in it. You can also toss lavender sachets into your drawers and garment bags and hang them in your closets.

KNIT CAFE
90069
★ ★ ★ ★

LALA SCARF
KAT COYLE

Mohair seems to be one of those fibers that you either love or hate. I LOVE IT! I love its ethereal quality. There is nothing more beautiful than a panel of lace mohair hanging in front of a window with the sun shining through it. I picked a silk-mohair blend for this scarf so it would be especially soft around the neck or even tied in your hair.

FINISHED MEASUREMENTS
Approximately 14" long (measured along center st) by 33" wide (measured across CO edge, including Ruffle)

YARN
Rowan Kidsilk Haze (70% super kid mohair / 30% silk; 229 yards / 25 grams)

Version 1: 1 ball each #606 candy girl (MC), #585 nightly (A), and #597 jelly (B)

Version 2: 1 ball each #581 meadow (MC), #582 trance (A), and #585 nightly (B)

Knit One, Crochet Too Douceur et Soie (65% baby mohair / 35% silk; 225 yards / 25 grams)

Version 3: 1 ball each #8401 butter (MC) and #8243 soft sunrise (A)

NEEDLES
One pair straight needles size US 10 (6 mm)

Change needle size if necessary to obtain correct gauge.

NOTIONS
Crochet hook size E/4 (3.5 mm), stitch markers

GAUGE
12 sts and 22 rows = 4" (10 cm) in Stockinette stitch (St st)

I do have a few tips for working with mohair:

＊ Use needles that have a good scooping tip (I like Bryspun needles).

＊ Use small, close movements to keep yarn from slipping off the needles.

＊ Use your pointer fingers to hold yarn on both needles.

Version 1 (left) and
Version 2 (right)

Version 3

SCARF

Using MC, CO 3 sts.

Establish Pattern

Row 1 (WS): Purl.

Row 2 (RS): K1-f/b, yo, k1, yo, k1-f/b – 7 sts.

Rows 3, 5, and 7: Purl.

Row 4: K1, k1-f/b, k1, yo, k1, yo, k1, k1-f/b, k1 – 11 sts.

Row 6: K3, place marker (pm), yo, k2, yo, pm, k1, pm, yo, k2, yo, pm, k3 – 15 sts.

Rows 8 and 10: K3, slip marker (sm), yo, knit to next marker, yo, sm, k1, sm, yo, work to next marker, yo, sm, k3 – 23 sts after Row 10.

Rows 9 and 11: Purl.

Row 12: K3, sm, [yo] twice, [k1, wrapping yarn 3 times around needle] to next marker, [yo] twice, sm, k1, sm, [yo] twice, [k1, wrapping yarn 3 times around needle] to next marker, [yo] twice, sm, k3 – 63 sts.

Row 13: Purl, slipping markers and dropping all second yo's and extra wraps – 27 sts remain.

*Repeat Rows 8 – 9 five times – 47 sts after last repeat. Repeat Rows 12 – 13 once – 51 sts after Row 13. Repeat from * once – 75 sts. Repeat Rows 8 – 9 five times – 95 sts. Break yarn.

RUFFLE

Note: If working Version 3, use A for entire Ruffle; do not change to B on Row 3.

Row 1: Using A, *k1, yo; repeat from * across to last st, k1-f/b – 190 sts.

Row 2: Purl.

Row 3: Change to B; *k1, yo; repeat from * across to last st, k1-f/b – 380 sts.

Row 4: Purl. Break yarn (Versions 1 and 2 only).

Work Picot Loops: *[Using Cable CO method (see Special Techniques, page 137) and A, CO 2 sts in front of first st on left-hand needle, BO 2 sts, slip remaining st back to left-hand needle] 4 times to make a chain of 4 picots, BO 7 sts, slip remaining st back onto left-hand needle; repeat from * across until 2 sts remain, [CO 2 sts in front of first st on left-hand needle, BO 2 sts, slip remaining st back onto left-hand needle] 4 times, BO 1 st; fasten off but do not break yarn.

FINISHING

Using crochet hook and yarn attached to picot loops BO, work 1 row sc loosely across shaped edges; fasten off. Weave in all loose ends. Block lightly on WS.

I LOVE YOUR aura

One afternoon, an older man and his wife came into the shop *and went straight to the sparkly Trendsetter Aura (a nylon yarn that looks like tinsel). They huddled over it for quite a long time discussing the colors. Finally, they came to the counter with about forty balls in a rainbow of colors. It turns out they own a fishing store in Canada and he makes and sells fish hooks made with the Aura, which sparkles in the water, attracting the fish to the hook. A few weeks later, I received these pretty hooks from them in the mail.*

LOVE BLANKET

I asked two customers to knit the panels for this blanket and because their gauges do not match exactly, each panel is a little "off." The edges are not quite as straight I had originally meant them to be but, frankly, *I love that!* I like to embrace imperfections and often find great humor and charm in them. And I like to believe that Knit Cafe is a place where people feel comfortable making mistakes. The blanket is perfect for the beach or picnics or reading by the fire. It is made of four garter-stitch panels. The letters are knit separately and sewn on.

FINISHED MEASUREMENTS
Approximately 42" wide by 80" long

YARN
Blue Sky Alpacas Blue Sky Cotton (100% cotton; 150 yards / 100 grams): 10 skeins each #608 lemonade (A) and #615 tulip (B), for Panels

Lana Grossa Leggero (100% polyamide; 178 yards / 50 grams): 2 balls #14 aqua (C), for Letters

Contrasting color of scrap yarn (cotton is best) for attaching Letters

NEEDLES
One 24" circular (circ) needle size US 8 (5 mm)

One 36" circular needle size US 8 (5 mm)

One pair straight needles size US 7 (4.5 mm)

NOTIONS
Crochet hook size H/7 (4.5 mm), yarn needle

GAUGE
17 sts and 28 rows = 4" (10 cm) in Garter stitch using larger needles and A

19 sts and 24 rows = 4" (10 cm) in Garter stitch using smaller needles and C

NOTE
If it is important to you that your panels are even and consistent in size, check your gauge approximately every 10".

YELLOW PANEL (make two)
Using shorter circ needle and A, CO 85 sts; begin Garter st. Working back and forth on needle, work even until piece measures 42" from beginning. BO all sts loosely.

WHITE PANEL (make two)
Using longer circ needle and B, CO 180 stitches; work as for Yellow Panel until piece measures 20" from beginning. BO all sts loosely.

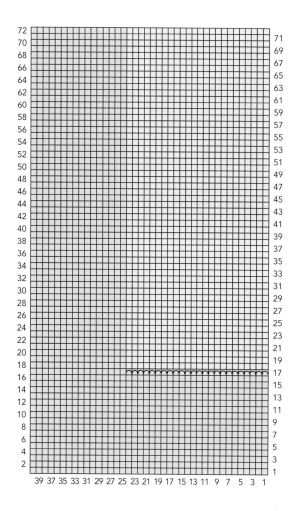

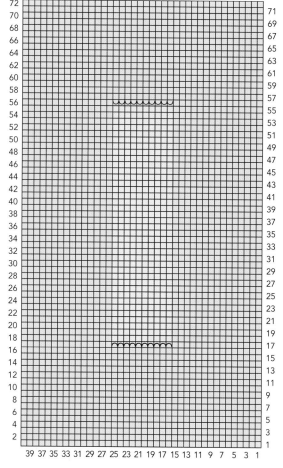

KEY

Knit all rows.

▨	C	⊠ (Ssk)	Ssk
☐	No stitch	◠	BO 1 st
⊠	M1	◡	CO 1 st
⊠	K2tog	🌢	Join second ball of yarn and work both sides at same time.

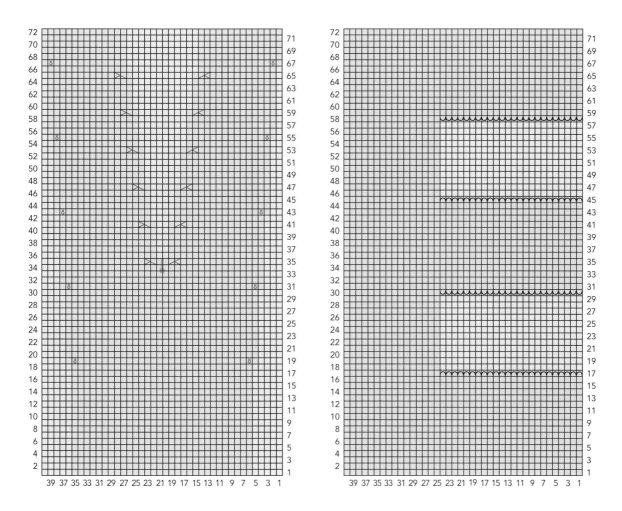

LETTER "L"

Note: When working Letters, you may work from the written instructions given, or from the chart for each Letter. If your row gauge does not match the gauge given, it is recommended that you work the Letters from the written instructions so that they will be the correct size and proportions.

Using smaller needles and C, CO 40 sts; begin Garter st. Work even until piece measures 3" from beginning, end with a WS row.

Next Row (RS): BO 24 sts, work to end – 16 sts remain.

Work even until piece measures 12" from beginning, end with a WS row. BO all sts loosely knitwise.

LETTER "O"

Using smaller needles and C, CO 40 sts; begin Garter st. Work even until piece measures 3" from beginning, end with a WS row.

Next Row (RS): K15, join a second ball of yarn and BO center 10 sts, work to end – 15 sts remain each side.

Working both sides at same time, work even until piece measures 9" from beginning, end with a RS row.

(WS) K15, CO 10 sts, work to end – 40 sts.

Work even until piece measures 12" from beginning, end with a WS row. BO all sts loosely knitwise.

LETTER "V"

Using smaller needles and C, CO 30 sts; begin Garter st. Work even until piece measures 3" from beginning, end with a WS row.

Shape Letter: (RS) Increase 1 st each side this row, then every 2" 4 more times, as follows: K1, m1, work to last st, m1, k1, and AT THE SAME TIME, when piece measures 5½" from beginning, Shape Center as follows: Work 17 sts, join a second ball of yarn and work to end – 17 sts each side. Working both sides at same time, continue increases at outside edges only as established and AT THE SAME TIME, decrease 1 st at each inside edge on next RS row, then every 1" 5 more times, as follows: on right side of "V", work to last 3 sts, k2tog, k1; on left side of "V", k1, ssk, work to end – 14 sts remain each side after completing all increases and decreases. Work even until piece measures 12" from beginning, end with a WS row. BO all sts loosely knitwise.

LETTER "E"

Using smaller needles and C, CO 40 sts; begin Garter st. Work even until piece measures 3" from beginning, end with a WS row.

Next Row (RS): BO 24 sts, work to end – 16 sts remain. Work even until piece measures 5" from beginning, end with a RS row.

Next Row: (WS) Work to end, CO 24 sts – 40 sts. Work even until piece measures 7½" from beginning, end with a WS row.

Next Row: (RS) BO 24 sts, work to end – 16 sts remain. Work even until piece measures 9½" from beginning, end with a RS row.

Next Row: (WS) Work to end, CO 24 sts – 40 sts. Work even until piece measures 12" from beginning, end with a WS row.

BO all sts loosely knitwise.

FINISHING

Using A, sew 4 Panels together along their long sides, beginning with a B Panel and alternating colors. Center "L" on first Panel (B) and pin in position. Repeat with "O", "V", and "E" on following Panels. Using scrap yarn and yarn needle, appliqué each Letter to its Panel using Blanket Stitch. Using yarn needle, weave in all loose ends.

FRINGE

For each Fringe, cut 3 18" lengths of A – 180 strands total (60 Fringes for A side). Attach Fringe (see Special Techniques, page 137) to short A end of blanket, approximately every 1". Repeat with B on opposite end of blanket. Trim fringe.

hand made

Angora, alpaca, mohair,
so many fibers.
This one sheds.
This one itches.
This one, delicate,
breaks if the tension is too much.

I CHOOSE YOU,
silk and wool.
the perfect mix of smooth and rough
against my skin.
Hand-dyed, variegated, chocolate brown,
cobalt blue, sage green,
rich, warm.

I try you out.
Knit a swatch.
Check the gauge.
My heart knit-purl, knit-purls the pattern.
You are skeins and skeins of possibility.

The air is chill, but
I look forward to Winter
I am making love.
Come to me,
I WANT TO WEAR YOU.

LUSH HOODIE
JULIA TRICE

Sweatshirts were originally created in the 1920s for athletes to wear for pre-game warmups. Before long, a zipper-front hooded sweatshirt called The Sideline was being worn by professional football players across the country. In recent years, fashion designers have borrowed the "hoodie" style from the sports world, expanding its popularity by slenderizing it and making it in luxurious fabrics and beautiful colors. This hoodie, which can be worn for play, work, and even an evening out, is knitted in a yummy blend of angora and wool called Lush.

SIZES
X-Small (Small, Medium, Large, X-Large)

To fit women's bust size 32 (34, 36, 38, 40)"

Shown in size X-Small.

FINISHED MEASUREMENTS
43 (45, 47, 49, 51)"

YARN
Classic Elite Lush (50% angora / 50% wool; 123 yards / 50 grams): 8 (10, 11, 13, 14) skeins #4420 aqua foam (MC)

NEEDLES
One pair straight needles size US 6 (4 mm)

One pair straight needles size US 7 (4.5 mm)

Change needle size if necessary to obtain correct gauge.

NOTIONS
Stitch markers, 18 (18, 18, 20, 20)" coordinating color separating zipper (zipper will show), sewing needle and thread, yarn needle, size G/6 (4 mm) crochet hook.

GAUGE
19 sts and 26 rows = 4" (10 cm) in Stockinette stitch (St st) using larger needles

Using smaller needles, CO 86 (90, 94, 98, 102) sts. Work in k2, p2 rib until piece measures 2½" from beginning, end with a WS row, as follows:

Row 1: (WS) K2, *p2, k2; repeat from * across.
Row 2: (RS) *P2, k2; repeat from * across to last 2 sts, p2.

Change to larger needles and St st; work even for 18 rows, end with a WS row.

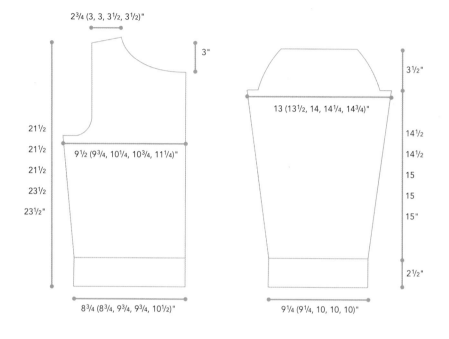

2¾ (3, 3, 3½, 3½)"

3"

21½
21½
21½
23½
23½"

9½ (9¾, 10¼, 10¾, 11¼)"

8¾ (8¾, 9¾, 9¾, 10½)"

13 (13½, 14, 14¼, 14¾)"

3½"
14½
14½
15
15
15"
2½"

9¼ (9¼, 10, 10, 10)"

Shape Sides: (RS) Increase 1 st each side on this row, then every 18 rows twice – 92 (96, 100, 104, 108) sts. Work even until piece measures 13 (12¾, 12¾, 14¼, 14¼)" from beginning, end with a WS row.

Shape Armholes: (RS) BO 3 (4, 4, 4, 5) sts at beginning of next 2 rows – 86 (88, 92, 96, 98) sts remain.

Decrease 1 st at each side every row 3 times, every other row 3 times – 74 (76, 80, 84, 86) sts remain. Work even until Armholes measure 7 (7¼, 7¼, 7¾, 7¾)" from beginning of shaping, end with a WS row.

Shape Neck: (RS) Work 19 (20, 21, 22, 23) sts; join second ball of yarn and BO next 36 (36, 38, 40, 40) sts, work to end. Working both sides at the same time, at each neck edge, BO 3 sts once, 2 sts once, then decrease 1 st on next WS row – 13 (14, 15, 16, 17) sts remain. Work even until Armhole measures 8 (8¼, 8¼, 8¾, 8¾)" from beginning of shaping, end with a WS row.

Shape Shoulders: (RS) At each Armhole edge, BO 6 (7, 7, 8, 8) sts once, 7 (7, 8, 8, 9) sts once.

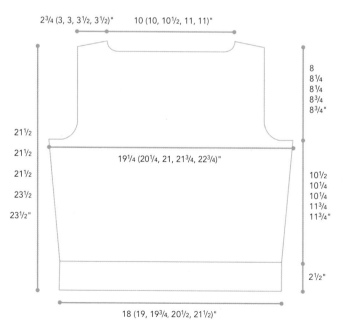

2¾ (3, 3, 3½, 3½)"   10 (10, 10½, 11, 11)"

8
8¼
8¼
8¾
8¾"

21½
21½
21½
23½
23½"

19¼ (20¼, 21, 21¾, 22¾)"

10½
10¼
10¼
11¾
11¾"

2½"

18 (19, 19¾, 20½, 21½)"

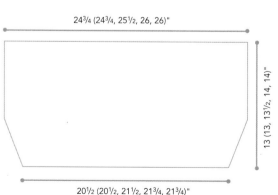

24¾ (24¾, 25½, 26, 26)"

13 (13, 13½, 14, 14)"

20½ (20½, 21½, 21¾, 21¾)"

LEFT FRONT

Using smaller needles, CO 42 (42, 46, 46, 50) sts. Begin in k2, p2 rib as for Back; work even until piece measures 2½" from beginning, increase 0 (2, 0, 2, 0) sts evenly across last (WS) row – 42 (44, 46, 48, 50) sts.

Change to larger needles and St st; work 18 rows, end with a WS row.

Shape Sides: (RS) Increase 1 st at beginning of this row, then every 18 rows twice – 45 (47, 49, 51, 53) sts. Work even until piece measures 13 (12¾, 12¾, 14¼, 14¼)" from beginning, end with a WS row.

Shape Armhole: (RS) BO 3 (4, 4, 4, 5) sts at beginning of this row – 42 (43, 45, 47, 48) sts remain. At Armhole edge, decrease 1 st every row 3 times, then every other row 3 times – 36 (37, 39, 41, 42) sts remain. Work even until Armhole measures 5 (5¼, 5¼, 5¾, 5¾)" from beginning, end with a RS row.

Shape Neck: (WS) At neck edge, BO 15 (15, 16, 17, 17) sts once, 3 sts once, 2 sts once, then decrease 1 st every other row 3 times – 13 (14, 15, 16, 17) sts remain. Work even until Armhole measures 8 (8¼, 8¼, 8¾, 8¾)" from beginning of shaping, end with a WS row.

Shape Shoulder: At Armhole edge, BO 6 (7, 7, 8, 8) sts once, 7 (7, 8, 8, 9) sts once.

RIGHT FRONT

Work as for Left Front, reversing all shaping.

SLEEVES (make two)

Using smaller needles, CO 42 (42, 46, 46, 46) sts. Begin in k2, p2 rib as for Back; work even until piece measures 2½" from beginning, increase 2 sts evenly across last (WS) row – 44 (44, 48, 48, 48) sts.

Change to larger needles and St st; work 8 rows even, end with a WS row.

Shape Sleeve: (RS) Increase 1 st each side on this row, then every 8 rows 8 (9, 8, 9, 7) times, then every 6 rows 0 (0, 0, 0, 3) times – 62 (64, 66, 68, 70) sts.

Work even until piece measures 17 (17, 17½, 17½, 17½)" from beginning, end with a WS row.

Shape Cap: (RS) BO 3 (4, 4, 4, 5) sts at beginning of next 2 rows – 56 (56, 58, 60, 60) sts remain. Decrease 1 st at each side every row 3 times, then every other row 3 times, then every 4 rows 3 times – 38 (38, 40, 42, 42) sts remain. BO remaining sts.

HOOD

Sew shoulder seams. With RS facing, using larger needles, pick up and knit 98 (98, 102, 104, 104) sts evenly around neck edge, place marker at center Back. Begin in St st with a purl row; work 3 rows even, end with a WS row.

Shape Hood, Increase Row: (RS) Work to 1 st before marker, m1, work 2 sts, m1, work to end. Work 3 rows even. Repeat Increase Row on this row, then every 4 rows 8 more times –118 (118, 122, 124, 124) sts. Work even until Hood measures 13 (13, 13½, 14, 14)" from pick-up row, ending with a WS row.

Place half of the stitches on one needle and the other half on the second needle. Fold Hood in half (WS of Hood is together) so that the needles are next to one another with points facing in the same direction. Using the Kitchener Stitch, graft sts together, or using Three-Needle Bind Off Method, BO all sts (see Special Techniques, page 137).

FINISHING

Set in Sleeves. Sew Sleeve and side seams. Using crochet hook, work chain st along center Front edges and Hood edge. Using yarn needle, weave in all loose ends. Sew in zipper.

PEACE PILLOW
MARY-HEATHER COGAR

Mary-Heather is the daughter of a free-spirited mother who packed her three kids and one cat into the family station wagon and moved them cross-country from Fairfax, Virginia, to the San Francisco Bay Area with just two weeks notice! It's only fitting that Mary-Heather became a hippie Deadhead theater major. Nowadays, she includes talented knitter on her resume. She designed this pillow for Knit Cafe.

FINISHED MEASUREMENTS
Approximately 12" wide by 11¼" high

YARN
Tahki Cotton Classic (100% mercerized cotton; 108 yards / 50 grams): 1 hank each #3803 blue (A), #3352 tiger lily (B), #3722 green (C), and #3532 yellow (D)

Tahki Tweedy Cotton Classic (100% mercerized cotton; 108 yards / 50 grams): 1 hank #467 red (E)

NEEDLES
One pair straight needles size US 6 (4 mm)

One pair double-pointed needles (dpn) size US 6 (4 mm)

NOTIONS
Yarn needle; five ¾" buttons; 12" pillow form or fiberfill

GAUGE
20 sts and 28 rows = 4" (10 cm) in Stockinette stitch (St st)

FRONT
Using straight needles and A, CO 60 sts; begin St st and Chart. Work even until Chart is completed; BO all sts loosely.

BOTTOM BACK
Using straight needles and A, CO 60 sts; begin St st, working Stripe Sequence as follows: 12 rows A, 2 rows B, 11 rows C, 2 rows B, 8 rows D. Change to E and Garter st; work even for 12 rows. BO all sts loosely knitwise.

TOP BACK
Work as for Bottom Back to end of Stripe Sequence. Change to E and Garter st; work even for 5 rows.

St st — knit on RS,
purl on WS

A B C D E

Buttonhole Row (RS): K8, BO 4 sts, [k6, BO 4 sts] 4 times, k8.

Next Row: K8, CO 4 sts over BO sts of previous row by working 4 firm Backward Loop CO's (see Special Techniques, page 137), [k6, CO 4 sts] 4 times, k8.

Work even in Garter st for 5 more rows. BO all sts loosely knitwise.

I-CORD EDGING

Using dpn and B, CO 3 sts; work I-cord (see page 137) until piece measures 44" from beginning. Leave sts on needle for finishing.

FINISHING

Pin Bottom Back to Front. Sew side and bottom seams, taking care to match stripes. Pin Top Back to Front, with Buttonhole Band overlapping Bottom Back at center. Sew side and bottom seams, taking care to match stripes. Pin I-cord to seams around pillow edges, adjusting length of I-cord as necessary; sew in place. Using Kitchener stitch (see page 137), graft live stitches of I-cord to CO row. Using yarn needle, weave in all ends. Sew on buttons opposite buttonholes.

POLO SHIRT
BETH ABARAVICH

The definition of a polo shirt, according to Webster's Unabridged Dictionary, is "a short-sleeved, usually knitted, pullover sport shirt for men and boys, somewhat like a T-shirt but generally with a collar." We kept this design pure for the most part, even including a longer shirttail in the back, but added soft shaping at the waist to flatter girlish figures.

SIZES
Small (Medium, Large, X-Large)

FINISHED MEASUREMENTS
36 (38, 40½, 42½)" chest

Shown in size Medium.

YARN
GGH Scarlett (100% Egyptian cotton; 114 yards / 50 grams): 7 (7, 8, 9) balls #29 celadon (MC); 1 ball #1 oyster (A)

NEEDLES
One pair straight needles size US 3 (3.25 mm)

One pair straight needles size US 5 (3.75 mm)

Change needle size if necessary to obtain correct gauge.

NOTIONS
Crochet hook size US D/3 (3.25 mm)

Row markers; stitch markers

GAUGE
21 sts and 28 rows = 4" (10 cm) in Stockinette stitch (St st) using larger needles

NOTES

Decrease Row: (RS) K2, ssk, work to last 4 sts, k2tog, k2.
Increase Row: (RS) K2, m1, work to last 2 sts, m1, k2.
Decrease Row: (WS) P2, p2tog, work to last 4 sts, p2tog-tbl, p2.
Increase Row: (WS) P2, m1p, work to last 2 sts, m1p, p2.

BACK
Using larger needles and MC, CO 95 (100, 106, 111) sts.

Establish Pattern
Hem Facing:
Row 1: (RS) K1, p1, work in St st to last 2 sts, p1, k1.
Row 2: P1, k1, work in St st to last 2 sts, k1, p1. Work even as established for 3 more rows.
Next Row (turning ridge): Knit.

Repeat Rows 1-2 for Hem Facing 7 times. Place row marker at beginning and end of row for side seams.

Shape Waist: (RS) Continuing in St st (omitting ribbed edge sts), work Decrease Row this row, then every 12 (14, 14, 10) rows 2 (2, 2, 3) times – 89 (94, 100, 103) sts remain. Work even until piece measures 1¾ (1¾, 2, 2)" from last Decrease Row, end with a WS row.

(RS) Work Increase Row this row, then every 12 (14, 14, 10) rows 2 (2, 2, 3) times – 95 (100, 106, 111) sts. Work even until piece measures 13¼ (14¼, 14¾, 15¼)" from turning row, end with a WS row.

Shape Armholes: (RS) BO 6 (7, 7, 8) sts at beginning of next 2 rows – 83 (86, 92, 95) sts remain.

Next Row: Work Decrease Row this row, then every other row 4 (6, 6, 6) times – 73 (72, 78, 81) sts remain. Work even until Armhole measures 7½ (7½, 8, 8)" from beginning of shaping, end with a WS row.

Shape Shoulders and Neck: (RS) BO 6 (6, 6, 7) sts at beginning of next 2 rows, 6 (6, 7, 7) sts at beginning of next 2 rows, then 7 (7, 7, 8) sts at beginning of next 2 rows. BO remaining 35 (34, 38, 37) sts for neck.

FRONT

Work as for Back until 8 rows have been completed after turning ridge, end with a WS row. Place row marker at beginning and end of row for side seams.

Work as for Back until piece measures 12¼ (13¼, 13¾, 14¼)" from turning row, end with a WS row – 95 (100, 106, 111) sts.

(RS) Shape Armholes as for Back AND AT THE SAME TIME, when Armhole measures 2¼ (2¼, 2¾, 2¾)" from beginning of shaping, end with a WS row.

Shape Placket: (RS) Mark center 7 (8, 8, 7) sts. Continue to Shape Armhole, work to first marker; join a second ball of yarn and BO center 7 (8, 8, 7) sts, work to end. Working both sides at same time, work even until Armhole measures 5¼ (5¼, 5¾, 5¾)" from beginning of shaping, end with a WS row – 33 (32, 35, 37) sts remain each side.

Shape Neck (RS): Working both sides at same time, at each neck edge, BO 5 (5, 6, 6) sts once, then decrease 1 st every other row 9 (8, 9, 9) times, AND AT THE SAME TIME, when Armholes measure same as Back to shoulder shaping, Shape Shoulders as for Back.

SLEEVES (make two)

Using larger needles and MC, CO 66 (68, 74, 76) sts; begin St st. Work 4 rows even, end with a WS row.

Hem Facing: (RS) Change to A and knit 2 rows (turning row).

Change to MC; work even in St st for 6 rows, end with a WS row.

Shape Sleeve: (RS) Increase 1 st each side on this row, then every row 7 (6, 0, 0) times, every other (RS) row 0 (1, 5, 4) times, every 4 rows 0 (0, 0, 1) time, working RS Increase Row or WS Increase Row as appropriate – 82 (84, 86, 88) sts.

Work even until piece measures 2 (2¼, 2½, 2¾)" from turning row, end with a WS row.

Shape Cap: (RS) BO 6 (7, 7, 8) sts at beginning of next 2 rows – 70 (70, 72, 72) sts remain. Decrease 1 st each side every other row 5 (6, 7, 7) times, every row 13 (12, 9, 9) times, then every other (RS) row 3 (3, 4, 4) times, working RS Decrease Row or WS Decrease Row as appropriate – 28 (28, 32, 32) sts remain. BO 3 (3, 4, 4) sts at beginning of next 4 rows – 16 sts remain. BO remaining sts.

FINISHING

Hem: On all pieces, fold hem to WS at turning ridge; stitch CO edge to WS of work. Sew shoulder seams. Set in Sleeves; sew Sleeve seams.

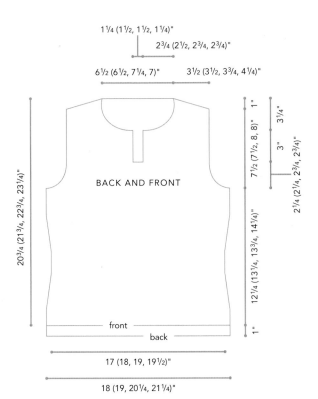

1 1/4 (1 1/2, 1 1/2, 1 1/4)"

2 3/4 (2 1/2, 2 1/2, 2 3/4)"

6 1/2 (6 1/2, 7 1/4, 7)"

3 1/2 (3 1/2, 3 3/4, 4 1/4)"

BACK AND FRONT

20 3/4 (21 3/4, 22 3/4, 23 1/4)"

7 1/2 (7 1/2, 8, 8)"

1"

3 1/4"

3"

2 1/4 (2 1/4, 2 3/4, 2 3/4)"

12 1/4 (13 1/4, 13 3/4, 14 1/4)"

1"

front

back

17 (18, 19, 19 1/2)"

18 (19, 20 1/4, 21 1/4)"

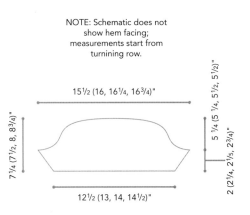

NOTE: Schematic does not show hem facing; measurements start from turning row.

15 1/2 (16, 16 1/4, 16 3/4)"

5 1/4 (5 1/4, 5 1/2, 5 1/2)"

7 1/4 (7 1/2, 8, 8 3/4)"

2 (2 1/4, 2 1/5, 2 3/4)"

12 1/2 (13, 14, 14 1/2)"

Right Placket

RS facing, using larger needles and MC, pick up and knit 7 (8, 8, 7) sts at base of Placket opening, CO 1 st – 8 (9, 9, 8) sts. Row 1 (WS): P0 (1, 1, 0), *k1, p1; repeat from * across. Row 2: *K1, p1; repeat from * across to last 0 (1, 1, 0) st, k0 (1, 1, 0). Work even as established until piece measures same as Placket opening. BO all sts in ribbing.

Left Placket

CO 8 (9, 9, 8) sts. Work as for Right Placket.

Sew left edge of Right Placket in place. Sew CO edge of Left Placket to pick-up ridge of Right Placket, on WS. Sew right edge of Left Placket in place.

Collar

WS facing, using smaller needles and MC, beginning 2 sts in from left Placket edge, pick up and knit 31 (32, 32, 33) sts around left Front neck edge, 34 (34, 38, 38) sts across Back neck edge, and 31 (32, 32, 33) sts around right Front neck edge, ending 2 sts in from right Placket edge – 96 (98, 102, 104) sts.

Row 1: (WS) P1, k1, work in St st (purl) to last 2 sts, k1, p1.
Row 2: K1, p1, work in St st (knit) to last 2 sts, p1, k1. Work 1 more row as established.
Shape Collar: (RS) Working in St st and continuing edge sts as established, work 7 (9, 11, 12) sts, k1-f/b, [k10,

k1-f/b] 8 times, work to end – 105 (107, 111, 113) sts. Work 3 rows even.

Next Row (RS): Work 8 (10, 12, 10) sts, k1-f/b, [k11, k1-f/b] 8 times, work to end – 114 (116, 120, 122) sts. Work 9 rows even. (RS) Change to A; knit 2 rows (turning ridge).

Hem Facing: (RS) Change to MC; work 4 rows in St st with edge sts. BO all sts loosely. Fold hem to WS at turning ridge; stitch BO edge to WS of work.

Pin sides together, beginning at row markers, and matching increase and decrease rows. Sew side seams. Using yarn needle, weave in all ends. Block to measurements.

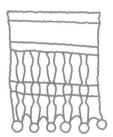

POMPOM AWNING *or shawl or table runner*
KAT COYLE

I just love it when something can have multiple purposes. The title of this project says it all. It is worked in two pieces and joined at the center back with a three-needle bind off. A crocheted edge finishes the two long sides and playful pompoms complete each of the lacy points (ten on each end).

FINISHED MEASUREMENTS
Approximately 70" long by 28" wide

YARN
Twisted Sisters Daktari Monochromatic Variegate (100% cotton, slubbed; 145 yards / 50 grams): 7 skeins #120165 gin blue (MC)

GGH Soft Kid (70% super kid mohair / 25% nylon / 5% wool; 150 yards / 25 grams): 2 skeins #028 dark pink

NEEDLES
Two 24" circular (circ) needles size US 7 (4.5 mm)

One pair straight needles size US 7 (4.5 mm)

One spare straight needle size US 7 (4.5 mm), for 3-needle bind off

Change needle size if necessary to obtain correct gauge.

NOTIONS
Row counter, yarn needle, size F/5 (3.75 mm) crochet hook, pompom maker (optional)

GAUGE
18 sts and 24 rows = 4" (10 cm) in Stockinette stitch (St st)

16 sts and 24 rows = 4" (10 cm) in Lace Pattern

NOTES
Maintain a 2-st Garter edge on each side of every row.

To avoid having to weave in lots of ends, carry both yarns along side of work and knit the first st of even-numbered (RS) rows with both yarns.

All odd-numbered (WS) rows are purled with the exception of maintaining the Garter st edges.

STITCH GUIDE
Lace Pattern (multiple of 12 sts + 5)

Row 1 and all odd-numbered rows (WS): K2, purl to last 2 sts, k2.
Rows 2, 4, and 6: K2, k2tog, *k2, yo, ssk, yo, k1, yo, k2tog, yo, k2, sl1-k2tog-psso; repeat from * across to last 13 sts, k2, yo, ssk, yo, k1, yo, k2tog, yo, k2, ssk, k2.
Row 8: K2, k2tog, *k1, yo, k2tog, yo, k3, yo, ssk, yo, k1, sl1-k2tog-psso; repeat from * across to last 13 sts, k1, yo, k2tog, yo, k3, yo, ssk, yo, k1, ssk, k2.

LACE CHART

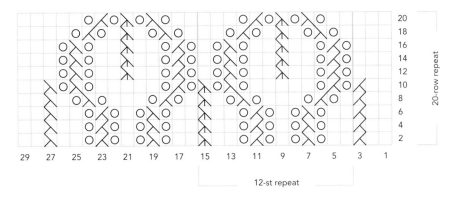

20
18
16
14
12
10
8
6
4
2

20-row repeat

29 27 25 23 21 19 17 15 13 11 9 7 5 3 1

12-st repeat

Row 10: K2, k2tog, *yo, k2tog, yo, k5, yo, ssk, yo, sl1-k2tog-psso*; repeat from * across to last 13 sts, yo, k2tog, yo, k5, yo, ssk, yo, ssk, k2.

Rows 12, 14, and 16: K3, *yo, k2tog, yo, k2, sl1-k2tog-psso, k2, yo, ssk, yo, k1; repeat from * across to last 14 sts, yo, k2tog, yo, k2, sl1-k2tog-psso, k2, yo, ssk, yo, k3.

Row 18: K4, *yo, ssk, yo, k1, sl1-k2tog-psso, k1, yo, k2tog, yo, k3 *; repeat from * across to last 13 sts, yo, ssk, yo, k1, sll1-k2tog-psso, k1, yo, k2tog, yo, k4.

Row 20: K5, *yo, ssk, yo, sl1-k2tog-psso, yo, k2tog, yo, k5 *; repeat from * across.

Repeat Rows 1–20 for Lace Pattern.

FIRST PANEL

Using MC and circ needle, CO 113 sts with Picot Point Cast-On Method (see Special Techniques, page 137).

Work 60 rows in Lace Pattern as follows:
Rows 1 to 21: MC; Rows 22 and 23: CC; Rows 24 to 31: MC; Rows 32 and 33: CC; Rows 34 to 59: MC; Row 60: CC.
Row 61: (WS) Using CC, k2, purl to last 2 sts, k2.

Work Rows 62 to 121 in St st stripes as follows:
Rows 62 to 67: MC; Rows 68 and 69: CC; Rows 70 to 89: MC; Rows 90 and 91: CC; Rows 92 to 97: MC; Rows 98 and 99: CC; Rows 100 to 111: MC; Rows 112 and 113: CC; Rows 114 to 119: MC; Rows 120 and 121: CC.
Rows 122 to 181: Repeat rows 2 to 61.
Rows 182 to 213: Repeat rows 62 to 93.

Cut yarn, leave sts on needle, and set aside.

SECOND PANEL

Using MC and second circ needle, CO 113 sts using Picot Point Cast-On Method.

Repeat Rows 1 to 189 as for First Panel.

Complete the final St st stripe section as follows:
Rows 190 to 201: MC; Rows 202 and 203: CC; Rows 204 to 207: MC.

Do not cut yarn.

FINISHING

With RS of panels held together, join panels together using Three-Needle Bind Off Method (see page 138). Using yarn needle, weave in all loose ends.

Work a crochet edging along the two long sides of the panel as follows:
With RS facing, CC, and crochet hook, *work 6 sc evenly across, ch 2, sc into last sc made *; repeat between * and * ending with 6 sc. Fasten off.

With three 90" long strands MC and two 90" long strands CC held together, make twenty 2" pompoms using a pompom maker or following instructions on page 138. Using MC, attach one pompom to each point on Panel's short sides.

RECYCLED SCARF
MARY-HEATHER COGAR

I asked Mary Heather to design a scarf with this cool, environmentally-conscious yarn and she came up with the idea of double-knitting it to showcase a different color on each side. This eight-ply yarn is spun from recycled cotton that originated as waste in the textile and apparel industry. Probably because it is made from recycled materials, it has a really interesting soft, bumpy texture that works well with its tweed palette.

FINISHED MEASUREMENTS
Approximately 62" long by 7" wide (after blocking)

YARN
Knit One Crochet Too 2nd Time Cotton (75% cotton / 25% acrylic; 180 yards / 100 grams): 2 balls each #120 Irish linen (A) and #142 glacier blue (B); 1 ball #273 Istanbul (pale red/ecru tweed; C)

NEEDLES
One 24" circular (circ) needle size US 8 (5 mm)

Change needle size if necessary to obtain correct gauge.

NOTIONS
2 stitch holders, yarn needle

GAUGE
18 sts and 23.5 rows = 4" (10 cm) in Stockinette stitch (St st)

STITCH GUIDE

Reversible Two-Color Double-Knitting
Row 1: Using B, *K1, slip 1 st wyif; repeat from * across. Slide sts back to beginning of needle.
Row 2: Using A, *slip 1 st wyib, p1; repeat from * across. Turn work.
Row 3: Using B, *slip 1 st wyib, p1; repeat from * across. Slide sts back to beginning of needle.
Row 4: Using A, *K1, slip 1 st wyif; repeat from * across. Turn work.

Repeat Rows 1–4 for pattern.

Note: When you begin to knit with B, bring yarn under A (as if you were joining a new color in intarsia work) in order to "link" the sides of scarf together.

Single-Color Double-Knitting
Row 1: Using C, *K1, slip 1 st wyif; repeat from * across. Turn work.

Repeat this Row for pattern.

Using A, CO 60 sts. Join B and work in Reversible Two-Color Double-Knitting for 88 rows (44 rows on each side of work), end on Row 4 of pattern. Distribute sts on two stitch holders, placing all A sts on one needle and all B sts on another holder.

*Join C and work in Single-Color Double-Knitting for 8 rows (4 rows on each side of work), carrying tails of A and B up side of scarf.

Work in Reversible Two-Color Double-Knitting for 8 rows (4 rows on each side of work), carrying C up side of scarf.

Work in Single-Color Double-Knitting for 16 rows, carrying A and B up side of scarf.

Work in Reversible Two-Color-Knitting for 8 rows, carrying C up side of scarf.

Work in Single-Color Double-Knitting for 8 rows. Cut C at end of final row, leaving an 8" tail to weave in.*

Work in Reversible Two-Color Double-Knitting until scarf measures 48" long from cast-on edge.

Repeat stripe pattern from * to *. Work in Reversible Two-Color Double-Knitting for 88 rows, until Scarf measures approximately 60" from beginning. Distribute sts on two stitch holders, placing all A sts on one holder and all C sts on another holder. Cut B, leaving a 6" tail to weave in. Carefully turn Scarf inside out and, using yarn needle, weave in all ends. Turn Scarf to right-side, and with B side of Scarf facing you, graft ends of scarf together using A and Kitchener stitch (see Special Techniques, page 137). Fasten off A and, using yarn needle, weave in remaining tail.

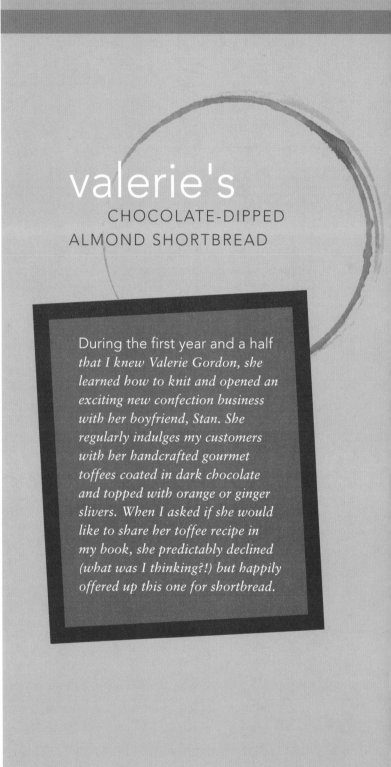

valerie's
CHOCOLATE-DIPPED ALMOND SHORTBREAD

During the first year and a half *that I knew Valerie Gordon, she learned how to knit and opened an exciting new confection business with her boyfriend, Stan. She regularly indulges my customers with her handcrafted gourmet toffees coated in dark chocolate and topped with orange or ginger slivers. When I asked if she would like to share her toffee recipe in my book, she predictably declined (what was I thinking?!) but happily offered up this one for shortbread.*

A Note from Valerie

This recipe was developed as a way to use leftover ingredients from our toffees. We always have some extra ingredients around the kitchen and luckily they transform into a variety of delicious cookies and confections. Quality ingredients truly make the difference between fair and delectable results. I encourage using the specific ingredients listed, though you may need to substitute for the sake of convenience and budget.

1¾ cups all-purpose flour
1½ cups ground organic almonds
¾ cup plus 1 tablespoon
    vanilla sugar (see Note)
¼ teaspoon salt
1½ teaspoons vanilla extract
¾ cup plus 2 tablespoons sweet
    Plugra butter, softened
12-16 ounces bittersweet
    Valrhona chocolate

Preheat oven to 350°F. Butter a 9"x 13" sheet pan and set aside. In a large bowl, combine flour, ground almonds, vanilla sugar, salt, and vanilla. Blend in softened butter.

Press the dough into the prepared pan. Using an offset spatula, level the surface. Bake for 25 minutes, rotating the pan twice. Reduce the heat to 300°F and continue baking until the shortbread turns golden brown, approximately 15 minutes.

Let cool in pan 2-3 minutes on a wire rack, then slice the shortbread 12 rows vertically and 6 rows horizontally. Cool completely.

Invert a sheet pan and line with waxed or parchment paper. As the cookies are cooling, melt the chocolate in the top of a double boiler, being careful to keep the temperature under 120°F, until smooth.

Dip the individual pieces of shortbread into the melted chocolate and place them on the lined sheet pan to set. You may want to drizzle the chocolate over the shortbread or spread the chocolate across the entire surface for a different look (and taste). At this point, it might be necessary to refrigerate the shortbread for 2-3 minutes.

Note: Vanilla sugar is the easiest thing to make! Place 2 whole vanilla beans (sliced in the center) in an airtight glass jar with 3-4 cups white sugar. Let sit in the cupboard for at least one week. If you don't have vanilla sugar, substitute granulated sugar.

Store in an airtight container for 2-3 days. Makes 6 dozen.

RED CARPET GOWN
KATHERINE LEE

From the start, I knew I wanted to include a beautiful gown in this book. Here in Los Angeles, it could be worn to the Oscars or to a formal wedding or New Year's Eve party. I met with Katherine, who has extensive experience designing knitted eveningwear, and we came up with this exquisite dress. It's knit in the most sumptuous silk yarn and has a lace border with a scalloped hem that swings as you walk. The icing on the cake was shooting this photograph at Erica Courtney's jewelry studio near Knit Cafe. When Erica isn't busy adorning stars with her signature pieces, she can often be found hanging out with us at the store, telling bawdy stories and crocheting awesome blankets.

SIZES
Small (Medium, Large)

Shown in size Small

FINISHED MEASUREMENTS
32 (33½, 36)" chest

YARN
Fiesta La Luz (100% silk; 210 yds / 2 oz): 7 (7, 8) hanks #3312 orchid

NEEDLES
One 32" (80 cm) circular (circ) needle size US 8 (5 mm)

One pair double-pointed needles (dpn) size US 8 (5 mm)

Change needle size if necessary to obtain correct gauge.

NOTIONS
Stitch markers; row markers; yarn needle

GAUGE
20 sts and 24 rows = 4" (10 cm) in Stockinette stitch (St st)

NOTES
Decrease Row: (RS) K2, skp, work to last 4 sts, k2tog, k2.

Cluster: *Slip number of sts indicated to right-hand needle purlwise wyib, yf*, slip the same sts back to left-hand needle, yb; repeat between * once.

PARASOL LACE PATTERN
(multiple of 22 sts plus 1)

Note: The st count varies from row to row. The original number of sts is restored on Row 13.

Row 1 (RS): K1, *yo, [k1-tbl, p3] 5 times, k1-tbl, yo, k1; repeat from * across.
Row 2: P3, *[k3, p1] 4 times, k3, p5; repeat from * across, end last repeat with p3.
Row 3: K1, *yo, k1-tbl, yo, [k1-tbl, p3] 5 times, [k1-tbl, yo] twice, k1; repeat from * across.

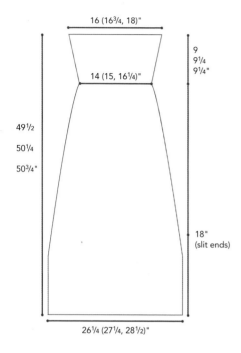

16 (16¾, 18)"

14 (15, 16¼)"

9
9¼
9¼"

49½
50¼
50¾"

18"
(slit ends)

26¼ (27¼, 28½)"

Row 4: P5, *[k3, p1] 4 times, k3, p9; repeat from * across, end last repeat with p5.

Row 5: K1, *yo, k1-tbl, yo, skp, yo, [k1-tbl, p2tog, p1] 5 times, k1-tbl, yo, k2tog, yo, k1-tbl, yo, k1; repeat from * across.

Row 6: P7, *[k2, p1] 4 times, k2, p13; repeat from * across, end last repeat with p7.

Row 7: K1, *k1-tbl, [yo, skp] twice, yo, [k1-tbl, p2] 5 times, k1-tbl, yo, [k2tog, yo] twice, k1-tbl, k1; repeat from * across.

Row 8: P8, *[k2, p1] 4 times, k2, p15; repeat from * across, end last repeat with p8.

Row 9: K2, *[yo, k2tog] twice, yo, k1-tbl, yo, [k1-tbl, p2tog] 5 times, [k1-tbl, yo] twice, [skp, yo] twice, k3; repeat from * across, end last repeat with k2.

Row 10: P10, *[k1, p1] 4 times, k1, p19; repeat from * across, end last repeat with p10.

Row 11: Skp, *[yo, k2tog] 3 times, k1-tbl, yo, [k1-tbl, p1] 5 times, k1-tbl, yo, k1-tbl, [skp, yo] 3 times, slip 2, k1, p2sso; repeat from * across, end last repeat with k2tog instead of slip 2, k1, p2sso.

Row 12: Repeat Row 10.

Row 13: K1, *[k2tog, yo] twice, k2tog, k1, k1-tbl, yo, [skp] twice, slip1-k2tog-psso, [k2tog] twice, yo, k1-tbl, k1, skp, [yo, skp] twice, k1; repeat from * across.

Row 14: Cluster 2, *p7, Cluster 5, p7, Cluster 3; repeat from * across, end last repeat with Cluster 2 instead of Cluster 3.

Repeat Rows 1–14 for Parasol Lace pattern.

TRELLIS LACE STITCH
(multiple of 2 sts plus 1)

Row 1 (RS): K1, *yo, k2tog; repeat from * across.
Row 2: Purl.
Row 3: *Skp, yo; repeat from * across to last st, k1.
Row 4: Purl.

Repeat Rows 1-4 for Trellis Lace st.

ZIGZAG LACE PANEL
(worked over 9 sts)

Row 1 (RS): K3, skp, yo, k2tog, yo, k2.
Row 2 and every WS row: Purl.
Row 3: K2, skp, yo, k2tog, yo, k3.
Row 5: K1, skp, yo, k2tog, yo, k4.
Row 7: Skp, yo, k2tog, yo, k5.
Row 9: Repeat Row 7.
Row 11: K2, yo, skp, yo, k2tog, k3.
Row 13: K3, yo, skp, yo, k2tog, k2.
Row 15: K4, yo, skp, yo, k2tog, k1.
Row 17: K5, yo, skp, yo, k2tog.
Row 19: Repeat row 17.
Row 20: Purl.

Repeat Rows 1-20 for Zigzag Lace panel.

EYELET STITCH
(worked over 2 sts)

Row 1 (RS): K2tog, yo.
Row 2: Purl.
Row 3: Yo, skp.
Row 4: Purl.

Repeat Rows 1-4 for Eyelet st.

FRONT

Using circ needle, CO 125 (133, 145) sts.

Establish Parasol Lace Pattern

Note: Slip all sts purlwise.

Row 1: (RS) Slip 1 st (selvage st – always work a slip 1 at beginning of row), [k1, p1] 3 (5, 8) times, place marker (pm), work Row 1 of Parasol Lace pattern over center 111 sts, pm, [p1, k1] 3 (5, 8) times, k1.

Row 2: Slip 1 st (selvage st), [p1, k1] 3 (5, 8) times, slip marker (sm), work Row 2 of Parasol Lace pattern to next marker, sm, [k1, p1] 3 (5, 8) times, k1.

Continuing in pattern as established, work even until 5 full repeats of Parasol Lace Pattern have been completed, end with a WS row (piece measures approximately 11½" from beginning, measured along edge).

Next Row (RS): Slip 1 st, [k1, p1] 3 (5, 8) times, sm, work in Garter st to next marker, sm, [p1, k1] 3 (5, 8) times, k1. Work even for 1 more row, working Garter st between markers.

Shape Skirt: (RS) Continuing in pattern as established, work to first marker, sm, k2, [k8, k2tog] 10 times, k9, sm, work to end – 115 (123, 135) sts remain. Work even for 2 rows.

Next Row: (WS) Work to first marker, sm, k2, [k7, k2tog] 10 times, k9, work to end – 105 (113, 125) sts remain. Work even for 2 rows.

Trellis Lace Panel

Next Row (RS): Slip 1 st, [k1, p1] 3 (5, 8) times, sm, work Row 1 of Trellis Lace st to next marker, sm, [p1, k1] 3 (5, 8) times, k1. Continuing in pattern as established, work even until 5 full repeats of Trellis Lace st have been completed, end with a WS row.

Next Row: (RS) Work to first marker, sm, k3tog, work to 3 sts before next marker, k3tog, sm, work to end – 101 (109, 121) sts remain. Work even for 7 rows. Place row marker at beginning and end of row for end of side slit (piece measures approximately 18" from beginning, measured along edge).

End Side Slit

(RS): K1 [omit selvage st], [skp] 1 (1, 3) times, k2, [skp] 1 (3, 4) times, sm, work as established to next marker, sm, [k2tog] 1 (3, 4) times, k2, [k2tog] 1 (1, 3) times, k1 – 97 (101, 107) sts remain. Work even for 11 rows keeping 5 (7, 10) sts at either end in St st, end with a WS row.

Next Row: (RS) Work to first marker, sm, k3tog, work to 3 sts before next marker, k3tog, sm, work to end – 93 (97, 103) sts remain. Work even for 11 rows, end with a WS row (piece measures approximately 21¾" from beginning, measured along edge).

Next Row: (RS) Change to St st, removing markers; work Decrease Row (see Notes) – 91 (95, 101) sts remain. Work even in St st for 11 rows. Work Decrease Row – 89 (93, 99) sts remain. Work even for 15 rows.

Parasol Lace Panel

Next Row (RS): K0 (2, 5), pm, work Row 1 of Parasol Lace pattern over center 89 sts, pm, k0 (2, 5). Work one full repeat of Parasol Lace pattern, end with a WS row.

(RS) Change to St st, removing markers, and work Decrease Row this row, then every 8 rows 3 times – 81 (85, 91) sts remain. Work even for 3 rows, end with a WS row.

Next Row (RS): K7 (9, 12), pm, work Row 1 of Parasol Lace pattern over center 67 sts, pm, k7 (9, 12). Work one full repeat of Parasol Lace pattern, and at the same time, work Decrease Row on next RS row, and every 6 rows once – 77 (81, 87) sts remain. Work even for 5 rows.

Next Row (RS): Change to St st. Work Decrease Row – 75 (79, 85) sts remain. Purl 1 row.

Bodice Lace Panels

(RS) K17 (18, 20), pm, work Row 1 of Eyelet st over 2 sts, pm, k14 (15, 16), pm, work Row 1 of Zigzag Lace panel over 9 sts, pm, k14 (15, 16), pm, work Row 1 of Eyelet st over 2 sts, pm, k17 (18, 20). Work even as established, working sts between patterns in St st, for 3 (7, 9) rows.

Shape Bodice: (RS) Work Decrease Row this row, then every 6 rows twice, every 8 rows once – 67 (71, 77) sts remain. Work even for 5 rows. (RS) Increase 1 st each side this row, then every 6 rows 3 times, then every

8 rows twice, as follows: K3, m1, work to last 4 sts, m1-r, k3 – 79 (83, 89) sts. Work even for 3 (3, 5) rows.

Note: Continue to work Eyelet sts as established. You will no longer work the Zigzag Lace panel; follow instructions as given.

Shape Keyhole Opening: (RS) Work to third marker, remove marker, k2tog, k2; join a second ball of yarn, BO 1 st, k2, ssk, remove marker, work to end – 38 (40, 43) sts remain each side. Working both sides at same time,

Rows 1, 3, 5, and 7 (WS): On right side, work to second marker, purl to end of side; on left side, slip 1 st (selvage st), purl to first marker, work to end.

Row 2: On left side, k3, m1, continue as established to last 4 sts, k2tog, k2; on right side, sl 1 (selvage st), k1, ssk, purl to first marker, sm, work to last 3 sts, m1, k3.

Row 4: Repeat Row 2 – 38 (40, 43) sts.
Row 6: On left side, work to last 4 sts, k2tog, k2; on right side, sl 1, k1, ssk, work to end – 37 (39, 42) sts remain each side.
Row 8: On left side, work to end; on right side, slip 1 st, work to end.
Row 9: Repeat Row 1.
Next Row (RS): K1 (1, 0), *p1, k1; repeat from * across to end of left side, removing all markers. For right side, *k1, p1; repeat from * across to last 1 (1, 0) st, k1 (1, 0). (WS) P1 (1, 0), *k1,

p1; repeat from * across to end of right side. For left side, *p1, k1; repeat from * across to last 1 (1, 0) st, p1 (1, 0). Work even for 2 rows. BO all sts in ribbing.

BACK

Work as for Front to end of Trellis Lace st, end with a WS row (piece measures approximately 21¾" from beginning, measured along edge) – 93 (97, 103) sts remain.

Shape Skirt: (RS) Change to St st and work Decrease Row, removing markers – 91 (95, 101) sts remain. Repeat Decrease Row every 12 rows once, every 30 rows once, every 8 rows 3 times, every 6 rows 6 (3, 3) times, every 9 rows 0 (1, 0) times, every 11 rows 0 (0, 1) time, every 6 rows 0 (2, 2) times, then every 8 rows once – 67 (71, 77) sts remain. Work even for 5 (6, 6) rows.

(RS) Increase 1 st each side this row, then every 6 rows 3 times, every 8 rows twice, as follows: K3, m1, work to last 4 sts, m1, k3 – 79 (83, 89) sts. Work even for 13 (13, 15) rows.

Next Row: (RS) K1, *p1, k1; repeat from * across to end. (WS) P1, *k1, p1; repeat from * across. Work even for 2 rows. BO all sts in ribbing.

FINISHING

RS facing, pin edges of dress together between side slit markers and top of ribbing at chest, matching rows as closely as possible. Sew side seams.

Keyhole Neck Edging: RS facing, pick up and k17 sts along edge of keyhole neck opening, starting below ribbed rows at left edge and working around to right edge of opening, ending just below ribbed rows. BO all sts purlwise. Sew ribbing edges together to close top of Keyhole.

Straps: Using dpn, CO 2 sts. [K1-f/b] twice – 4 sts. Purl 1 row. Work I-cord (see Special Techniques, page 137) until piece measures 24 (24½, 25)" from beginning (stretch first to "set" sts, then release and measure) or to desired length. Fold strap in half. Insert folded end into keyhole neck opening and draw ends through to secure in position. Try on dress and mark positions for ends of straps on top edge of Back, approximately ⅓ of the width in from each edge, adjusting length and position as necessary. Using yarn needle, weave in all ends. Block to shape as necessary by lightly spraying garment with water and allowing it to air dry; DO NOT PRESS with iron, as this will permanently flatten the silk fabric. Dry clean only.

SLOUCHY CARDIGAN
HELENE ROUX

This is the perfect sweater to wear with your pajamas, especially on those mornings when you have to take the kids to school but don't feel like getting dressed. It's the sweater you wear on Sundays curled up with the newspaper or while cutting flowers in your garden on cool mornings. The flared sleeves and curly sides keep it pretty and feminine and the DK weight alpaca, worked at a slightly larger than usual gauge, keeps it light and cozy.

SIZES
Small/Medium (Medium/Large)

To fit women's bust size 32"-34" (34"-36")

Shown in size Medium/Large

FINISHED MEASUREMENTS
34 (35)"

YARN
Twisted Sisters Hand-Dyed Avarice (100% alpaca; 145 yards / 50 grams): 8 (9) skeins in lilac

NEEDLES
One pair straight needles size US 8 (5 mm) needles

Change needle size if necessary to obtain correct gauge.

NOTIONS
Stitch markers, yarn needle

GAUGE
19 sts and 25 rows = 4" (10 cm) in Stockinette stitch (St st)

BACK

CO 84 (88) sts

Row 1: (WS) *K1, p1; rep from * across.

Change to St st; work even until piece measures 4" from beginning, end with a WS row.

Shape Sides: (RS) Decrease 1 st each side on this row – 82 (86) sts remain

Work even until piece measures 8" from beginning, end with a WS row.

Decrease 1 st each side on this row – 80 (84) sts remain.

Work even until piece measures 16½" from beginning, end with a WS row.

Shape Armholes: (RS) BO 3 sts at beginning of next 2 rows, 2 sts at beginning of next 4 rows – 66 (70) sts remain. Decrease 1 st each side every row 3 times – 60 (64) sts remain.

Work even until Armhole measures 9½" from beginning of shaping, ending with a WS row.

Shape Shoulders: (RS) BO 5 sts at beginning of next 4 rows, 4 (6) sts at beginning of next 2 rows – 32 sts remain. BO remaining sts.

RIGHT FRONT
CO 84 (88) sts.

Row 1: (WS) *K1, p1; rep from * across.

Change to St st and AT THE SAME TIME, Shape Center Front as follows:

BO 2 sts at beginning of next row, then every other row 4 times. Work 1 (WS) row even. 74 (78) sts remain.

(RS) Decrease 1 st at beginning of this row, then every other row 23 times – 50 (54) sts remain, then every 4 rows 9 times, then every 6 rows 6 (8) times, AND AT THE SAME TIME, when the piece measures 16½" from beginning, shape Armhole.

Shape Armhole: (WS) At Armhole edge, BO 3 sts once, 2 sts twice, then decrease 1 st every row 3 times – 24 (26) sts remain.

Work until Armhole measures 9½" from beginning of shaping, end with a RS row.

Shape Shoulder: (WS) At Armhole edge, BO 5 sts twice, then 4 (6) sts once – 10 sts remain. Work 1 row even. BO remaining sts.

LEFT FRONT
Work as for Right Front, reversing all shaping.

SLEEVES (make two)
CO 61 (64) sts.

Row 1: (WS) *K1, p1; rep from * to last 1(0) st, k1 (0).

Change to St st; work 4 rows even, end with a WS row.

Shape Sleeve:
(RS) Decrease Row: [K10, k2tog] twice, k13 (16), [k2tog, k10] twice – 57 (60) sts remain.

Work 7 rows even, end with a WS row.

Decrease Row: [K9, k2tog] twice, k13 (16), [k2tog, k9] twice – 53 (56) sts remain

Work 7 rows even, end with a WS row.

Decrease Row: [K8, k2tog] twice, k13 (16), [k2tog, k8] twice – 49 (52) sts remain.

Work 7 rows even, end with a WS row.

Decrease Row: [K7, k2tog] twice, k13 (16), [k2tog, k7] twice – 45 (48) sts remain.

Work even in St st until piece measures 14 (13)" from beginning, end with a WS row.

Shape Sleeve: (RS) Increase 1 st each side on this row, then every 6 rows twice, every 4 rows 2 (4) times – 55 (62) sts.

Work even until piece measures 18" from beginning, ending with a WS row.

Shape Cap: (RS) BO 3 sts at beginning of next 2 rows, 2 sts at beginning of next 4 rows, then at each side decrease 1 st every other row 10 times – 21 (28) sts remain. Bind off remaining sts.

HOOD (optional)
CO 124 sts.

Row 1: (WS) *K1, p1; rep from * across.

Change to St st; work even until piece measures 9½" from beginning, end with a WS row.

Divide Hood and Shape Top: (RS) Work 62 sts, join second ball of yarn, work to end. Working both sides at the same time, work 1 (WS) row even.

Decrease 1 st at beginning of this row, then every other row once.

Work 2 rows even, end RS row.

Decrease Row: (RS) Decrease 1 st each side as follows: For Right Side of Hood, work across to last 3 sts, k2tog, work 1 st; for Left Side of Hood, work 1 st, ssk, work to end – 61 sts remain each side. Work 1 (WS) row. Repeat Decrease Row once, then at each center edge, BO 2 sts twice, 3 sts once, then 4 sts once, AND AT THE SAME TIME, at each outside edge, BO 7 sts twice, then 8 sts once.

BO remaining 27 sts each side.

FINISHING
Sew shoulders together. Set in Sleeves; sew side and Sleeve seams. Sew center back seam of Hood. Sew Hood to neck edge, lining up center back seam of hood with center Back neck edge. Using yarn needle, weave in all loose ends.

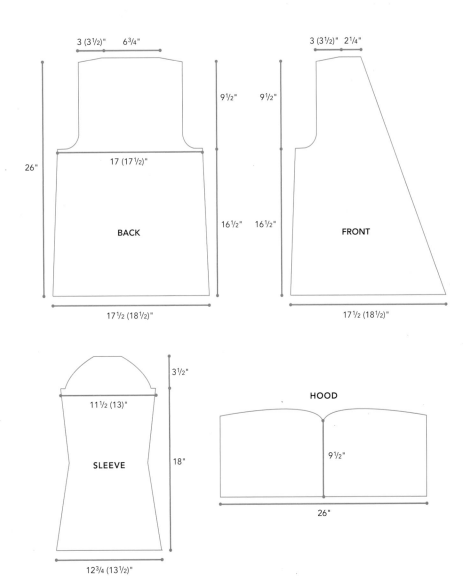

TERRY BATHROBE
DEENA WILLIAMS

This bathrobe is made with a synthetic chenille yarn that has an uncanny similarity to terry cloth. I was intrigued by it the first time I saw it and knew I wanted to use it to knit a classic terry cloth item. I asked Deena to design a robe for little kids to wear after a bath, or over pajamas or a bathing suit.

SIZE
To fit 3- to 5-year-old child

FINISHED MEASUREMENTS
Chest: 30"
Shoulder to Hem: 24"

YARN
Lana Grossa Leggero (100% microfiber; 178 yards / 50 grams): 5 balls #042 blue (MC) and 1 ball #029 orange (A)

NEEDLES
One pair straight needles size US 8 (5 mm)

Change needle size if necessary to obtain correct gauge.

NOTIONS
Yarn needle, pins, size G/6 (4 mm) crochet hook (for trim)

GAUGE
16 sts and 28 rows = 4" (10 cm) in Stockinette stitch (St st)

BACK
With MC, CO 60 sts; begin in St st. Work even until piece measures 17" from beginning, end with a WS row.

Shape Armholes: (RS) BO 3 sts at beg of next 4 rows, then at each side decrease 1 st once – 46 sts remain.

Work even until Armhole measures 7" from beginning of shaping, end with a WS row.

Shape Shoulders: (RS) BO 6 sts at beginning of next 2 rows, 5 sts at beginning of next 2 rows – 24 sts remain for Back neck. BO remaining sts.

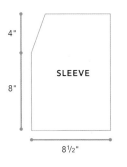

SLEEVE

4"

8"

8½"

11½"

3"

HOOD

11"

6½"

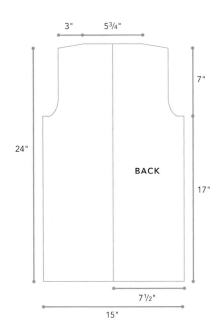

3" 5¾"

7"

24"

BACK

17"

7½"

15"

LEFT FRONT

Using MC, CO 30 sts; begin in St st. Work even until piece measures 17" from beginning, end with a WS row.

Shape Armhole: (RS) At Armhole edge, BO 3 sts twice, then decrease 1 st once – 23 sts remain.

Work even until Armhole measures 7" from beginning of shaping, end with a WS row.

Shape Shoulders as for Back at beginning of RS rows only – 12 sts remain. BO remaining sts.

RIGHT FRONT

Work as for Left Front, reversing all shaping.

SLEEVES (make two)

Using MC, CO 26 sts; begin in St st. Work even until piece measures 1½" from beginning, end with a WS row.

Shape Sleeve: (RS) Increase 1 st at each side on this row, then every 4 rows 3 times, every 6 rows 6 times – 46 sts.

Work even until piece measures 11" from beginning, end with a WS row.

Shape Cap: (RS) BO 3 sts at beg of next 4 rows, then at each side decrease 1 st every other row 8 times – 18 sts remain.

BO 4 sts at beg of next 2 rows – 10 sts remain. BO remaining sts.

HOOD

First Side: Using MC, CO 26 sts; begin in St st. Work even until piece measures 8" from beginning, end with a WS row.

Shape Hood: (RS) Decrease 1 st at beginning of this row, then every 4 rows 5 times – 20 sts remain.

Work even until piece measures 12" from beginning, end with a WS row. BO all sts.

Second Side: Work as for First Side of Hood, reversing all shaping, by decreasing at the end of RS rows.

BELT

Using MC, CO 8 sts; begin in Garter st. Work even until piece measures 42" from beginning, AND AT THE SAME TIME, work Stripe Sequence as follows:

Work 3" using MC, 1" using A, 1" using MC, 2" using A, 28" using MC, 2" using A, 1" using MC, 1" using A, 3" using MC.

BO all sts.

FINISHING

Sew shoulder seams, leaving 12 sts at each front edge free. Sew Hood seam, leaving cast-on edges free. Sew cast-on edges of Hood around the neck edge. Set in Sleeves; sew side and Sleeve seams. Using yarn needle, weave in all loose ends.

Crochet Edging: With RS facing, using crochet hook and A, work 1 row of single crochet around center Front and Hood edges, then work 1 round of single crochet around lower edge of Sleeves. Fasten off.

WEHO BIKINI
(or West Hollywood)
JULIA TRICE

I found it pretty easy to enlist my customers to model all the projects in this book—except for this one. For some reason, no one volunteered. Despite being unwilling to model it, Julia said she thoroughly enjoyed knitting it. She got great satisfaction watching the colors of the self-striping yarn reveal themselves and seeing the small stitches form the fabric. Even though it's knit at 8 stitches to the inch, it still goes quickly given its itty-bittiess. If you're not a bikini wearer yourself, try making it for a friend.

SIZES
Small (Medium, Large)

FINISHED MEASUREMENTS
Bottom (hips): Hips 33"
(35", 37")
Top (bust): Bust 32 (34", 36")
Shown in size Small

YARN
Lana Grossa Meilenweit Cotton Multiringel (45% cotton / 42% wool / 13% polymide; 415 yards / 100 grams): 2 skeins #2210 multicolored

Rainbow Knitting Elastic, size 1 mm fine; 50 yards: 2 cards #02 white (or coordinating color)

NEEDLES
One 24" circular needle size US 1 (2.5 mm)

One pair straight needles size US 1 (2.5 mm), for top straps (optional)

Change needle size if necessary to obtain correct gauge.

NOTIONS
Stitch markers, yarn needle

GAUGE
32 sts and 43 rows = 4" (10 cm) in Stockinette stitch (St st)

NOTE
Pieces are worked flat, but the length of the circular needle is needed to accommodate the number of stitches required for ties.

Bikini bottom is knit in one piece from top edge of front to top edge of back, starting with the front ties and ending with the back ties.

Bikini top is knit in one piece from bottom edge of front to the ties at neck.

BOTTOM
Front Ties: Using circular needle, CO 300 (340, 380) sts, placing stitch markers at even intervals, to track your stitch count as you cast on and to aid with proper count later.

Knit 1 row even.

At beginning of 2nd row, tie knitting elastic to the working yarn, leaving a 6" tail.

Knit 4 rows with the yarn and elastic held together, keeping the elastic at the same tension as the yarn, neither pulling too tightly nor leaving it loose.

At the end of 4th row, break off the knitting elastic, again leaving a 6" tail.

Knit 1 row even, using working yarn only.

Next Row (RS): Using stitch markers as a guide to stitch count and removing them as you work, BO 116 (134, 152) sts knitwise, k2 (total of 3 sts on right-hand needle), p62 (66, 70), k3, BO 116 (134, 152) sts knitwise – 68 (72, 76) sts remain. Cut yarn, leaving a 6" tail.

Bottom Front: With circular needle, rejoin yarn to live sts and work as follows:

Row 1: Knit.
Row 2: K3, p to last 3 sts, k3.
Row 3: K4, k2tog, k to last 6 sts, ssk, k4.
Row 4: K3, p to last 3 sts, k3.
Row 5: Knit.
Row 6: K3, p1, ssp, p to last 6 sts, p2tog, p1, k3.

Repeat these 6 rows 10 times – 24 (28, 32) sts.

Note: It is helpful to place st markers 4 sts in on each side of work to track where the decreases take place.

Sizes Medium and Large Only:
Row 1: Knit.
Row 2: K3, p1, ssp, p to last 6 sts, p2tog, p1, k3.

Repeat these 2 rows (1, 2) time(s) – (24, 26) sts remain.

All sizes:

Crotch: Work without decreasing, as follows:

Row 1: Knit.

Row 2: K3, p to last 3 sts, k3.

Repeat these 2 rows 14 times [30 rows] – 24 (24, 26) sts.

Bottom Back: Increase every RS row as follows:

Row 1: K4, m1 (right-leaning), k to last 6 sts, m1 (left-leaning), k4.

Row 2: K3, p to last 3 sts, k3.

Repeat these 2 rows 40 (42, 43) times – 106 (110, 114) sts.

Repeat Row 1 once – 108 (112, 116) sts.

Back Ties: (WS) CO 96 (114, 132) sts using the Knit-On Cast-On Method (see Special Techniques, page 137), then knit 96 (114, 132) sts, k3, p to last 3 sts, k3.

Next Row: (RS) CO 96 (114, 132) sts using the Knit-On Cast-On Method, then knit across all sts – 300 (340, 380) sts.

At the beginning of next (WS) row, tie knitting elastic to the working yarn, leaving a 6" tail.

Knit 4 rows with the yarn and elastic held together, keeping the elastic at the same tension as the yarn, neither pulling too tightly nor leaving it loose.

At the end of the 4th row, break off the elastic, again leaving a 6" tail.

Knit 1 row even, using working yarn only.

BO all sts knitwise, leaving a 6" tail.

FINISHING

Using yarn needle, weave in all loose ends of yarn and elastic.

TOP

Bust Tie: Using circ needle, CO 300 (340, 380) sts, placing stitch markers at even intervals to track your stitch count as you cast on and to aid with proper count later.

Knit 1 row even.

At beginning of second row, tie knitting elastic to the working yarn, leaving a 6" tail.

Knit 4 rows with the yarn and elastic held together, keeping the elastic at the same tension as the yarn, neither pulling too tightly nor leaving it loose.

At the end of 4th row, break off the knitting elastic, again leaving a 6" tail.

Knit 1 row even, using working yarn only.

Next Row: (RS) Using stitch markers as a guide to stitch count and removing them as you work, BO 103 (119, 135) sts knitwise, k2 (total of 3 sts on right-hand needle), p40 (44, 48), k3, BO 2 sts knitwise (center front), k2 (total of 3 sts on right-hand needle after last bind-off), p40 (44, 48), k3, BO 103 (119, 135) sts knitwise. Cut yarn, leaving a 6" tail. 92 (100, 108) sts remain – 46 (50, 54) sts for each Cup.

CUPS AND STRAPS

Note: Cups should be worked one at a time from the same skein to prevent variations in color. Once the first Cup is complete, work the second starting at the same point in the yarn color sequence as with the first.

Row 1 (WS): K3, p to last 3 sts, k3.

Row 2: Knit.

Row 3: K3, p to last 3 sts, k3.

Row 4: K4, k2tog, k to last 6 sts, ssk, k4.

Repeat these 4 rows 17 (19, 21) times – 10 sts remain.

Repeat Rows 1 – 3.

Next Row: K3, k2tog, ssk, k3 – 8 sts remain.

Repeat Rows 1 – 3.

Next Row: K2, k2tog, ssk, K2 – 6 sts remain.

Change to straight needles, if desired, and work Strap in Garter stitch, until Strap measures 11" (12", 13") from beginning.

Work second Cup as above.

FINISHING

Using yarn needle, weave in all loose ends of yarn and elastic.

YARMULKE
JENNY WHITE

West Hollywood is home to a vibrant community of immigrant Russian Jews, so we get frequent requests for yarmulke patterns. In modern congregations, yarmulkes can be worn by boys, girls, men, and women. This pattern knits up into a beautiful yarmulke for any occasion.

FINISHED MEASUREMENTS
Approximately 6½" diameter

YARN
Koigu Painter's Palette Premium Merino (KPPPM) (100% merino wool; 175 yards / 50 grams): 1 skein #P429

NEEDLES
One 16" circular (circ) needle size US 2 (2.75 mm)

One 16" circular (circ) needle size US 3 (3.25 mm)

One set of four double-pointed needles (dpn) size US 3 (3.25 mm)

Change needle size if necessary to obtain correct gauge.

NOTIONS
Yarn needle

GAUGE
28 sts and 42 rows = 4" (10 cm)

NOTES
Central Chain Decrease (CCD):
Slip next 2 sts knitwise as if to knit together, k1, pass slipped stitches over (psso). This decrease makes 1 stitch out of 3.

Wrap and Turn (w&t): Bring yarn to front if knitting (to back if purling), slip next st as if to purl, bring yarn to back if knitting (to front if purling), pass slipped stitch back to left-hand needle, turn work.

Knit wrap and wrapped stitch together (kwtog): pick up wrap knitwise (from underneath in the front) and knit it together with the wrapped stitch.

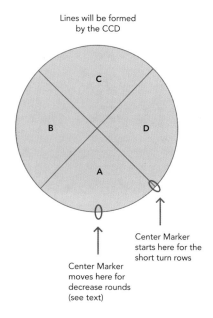

Lines will be formed
by the CCD

C

B   D

A

Center Marker
starts here for the
short turn rows

Center Marker
moves here for
decrease rounds
(see text)

Using smaller circ needles, CO 100 sts. Join for working in the rnd, being careful not to twist sts; place marker (pm) for the beginning of rnd.

Work 6 rnds in Garter st (k1 rnd, p1 rnd).

Change to larger circ needles and knit one rnd.

Next row is made of 4 sets of Short Rows, referred to as sections A, B, C, and D (see diagram):

K23, w&t, p21, w&t (do not wrap this st too tightly as it will be picked up from a more difficult angle than the wraps on the knit side), k19, w&t, p17, w&t (not too tightly), k17, [kwtog, k1] twice (the wraps at the other end of the short row sections will be picked up in the next round).

Repeat between * to * 3 times more for remaining sections B, C, and D.

Next rnd: *K1, kwtog, k1, kwtog, k21; repeat from * 3 times more (picking up wraps not yet picked up).

Remove center marker, k13, pm. This will now be the center marker.

Next Rnd: K11, [k2tog, k23] 3 times, k2tog, k12 – 96 sts remain.

Next Rnd: Knit.

Next Rnd: K10, [CCD, k21] 3 times, CCD, k11 – 88 sts remain.

Note: It may help to place a marker after each CCD. On the decrease round, slip 2 sts before marker, remove marker, knit the next stitch, psso and pm (make sure to use a different color

for the decrease markers than you did for the center marker).

Next rnd: Knit.

Next Rnd: K9, [CCD, k19] 3 times, CCD, k10 – 80 sts remain.

Next Rnd: Knit.

Continue in this manner (work 1 rnd with CCD's, and one rnd even) changing to US 3 dpn when necessary, until 16 sts remain.

FINISHING

Break yarn, thread tail through remaining 16 sts and pull tightly. Using yarn needle, weave in all loose ends.

WHAT WOULD
laura ingalls do?

When a customer comes into Knit Cafe *desperate because she's having trouble with her knitting (or I find her on the sidewalk pacing when I arrive to open the store for the day), I will often say, "First, take a deep breath. Now ask yourself: What would Laura Ingalls do?" I mean, there she was, out on the prairie, without a local yarn store, without* Vogue Knitting: The Ultimate Knitting Book, *without* Knitty.com. *What would she do? She would listen to her instincts and try to fix the problem in whatever way she could.*

YOGA MAT BAG
MARY-HEATHER COGAR

Both knitting and yoga naturally complement the relaxed and creative lifestyle so many enjoy in California. Around Knit Cafe it seems like there is a yoga studio on almost every block, and many of my customers are either yoga students or instructors. This yoga mat bag is knit in a sunny yellow-orange cotton yarn that is easy to wash. It also features a handy pocket on the front strap large enough for keys and money for class. The drawstring closure and hand-stitching along the strap and pocket edges give it a finished look.

FINISHED MEASUREMENTS
Bag: Approximately 16" circumference by 23" long

Strap: 25" long by 4" wide

YARN
Rowan All Seasons Cotton (60% cotton / 40% microfiber; 98 yds / 50 g): 6 balls #210 keen (orange and ecru multi; MC)

Rowan Wool Cotton (50% cotton / 50% wool: 123 yards / 50 grams): 1 ball each #900 antique (A; ecru) and #960 laurel (B; green)

NEEDLES
One 16" circular (circ) needle size US 6 (4 mm)

One set of 4 double-pointed needles size US 6 (4 mm)

Change needle size if necessary to obtain correct gauge.

NOTIONS
Stitch markers, yarn needle, 2 small buttons

GAUGE
19 sts and 26 rows = 4" in basketweave stitch using MC.

STITCH GUIDE

BASKETWEAVE PATTERN
(multiple of 16 sts; worked in the round)

Rnd 1 and every alternate rnd: Knit.
Rnds 2, 4, 6, 8, and 10: *K8, p8; repeat from * around.
Rnds 12, 14, 16, 18, and 20: *P8, k8; repeat from * around.

Repeat Rnds 1 – 20 for Basketweave pattern.

GARTER STITCH
(worked in the round)
Rnd 1: Purl
Rnd 2: Knit
Repeat Rnds 1 and 2.

BAG
Using MC and circular needle, CO 80 sts. Join for working in the rnd, being careful not to twist sts; place marker (pm) for beginning of rnd. Work 15 rnds in Garter stitch.

Rnd 16 (Eyelet Rnd): *K6, yo, k2tog; repeat from * around.

Change to Garter stitch; work 4 rnds.

Change to Basketweave pattern; work even until Bag measures approximately 25" long, end with Rnd 20 of Basketweave pattern.

Turning Ridge: Knit 1 rnd, then purl 2 rnds.

Shape Bottom as follows:
Decrease Rnd 1: *K16, pm; repeat from * around.

Rnd 2: *Ssk, k to 2 sts before marker, k2tog; repeat from * around – 70 sts remain

Rnd 3: Knit, distributing sts evenly on three dpns.
Rnd 4: Knit.
Rnd 5: *Ssk, k to 2 sts before marker, k2tog; repeat from * around – 60 sts remain.
Rnds 6-7: Knit.
Rnd 8: *Ssk, k to 2 sts before marker, k2tog; repeat from * around – 50 sts remain
Rnd 9: Knit.

Repeat Rnds 8 and 9 three more times – 20 sts remain.

Next Rnd: [Ssk, k2tog] 5 times – 10 sts remain.
Next Rnd: [K2tog] 5 times – 5 sts remain.

Cut yarn, leaving an 8" tail. Thread tail through remaining sts and pull tightly to secure.

STRAP
Note: Work strap back and forth on circ needle or switch to a straight needle.

Using MC and circ needle, CO 20 sts.

Row 1 and every (RS) row: Knit.
Rows 2, 4, and 6: K2, [k4, p4] twice, k2.
Rows 8, 10, and 12: K2, [p4, k4] twice, k2.

Repeat Rows 1-12 until Strap measures 30" from beginning. BO all sts.

I-CORD DRAWSTRING
Using dpn and A, CO 3 sts. Knit the first row. *Without turning the needles, slide the sts back to the other side of the needle; pull the yarn tight and knit the next row. Repeat from * until I-Cord measures 30" from beginning. BO all sts.

POCKET
Note: Work pocket back and forth on circ needle or change to a straight needle.

Using A, CO 18 sts; begin in St st. Work 2 rows even, end with a WS row.

Row 3: K2, m1, k to last 2 sts, m1, k2.
Row 4: Purl.
Row 5: K2, m1, k to last 2 sts, m1, k2 – 22 sts.

Work even in St st until piece measures 3½" from beginning, end with a WS row.

Knit 3 rows.

Next Row (Buttonhole Row): K6, yo, ssk, k6, k2tog, yo, k6.

Knit 3 rows.

BO all sts.

FINISHING
Using two strands of B held together, work Running Stitch embroidery just inside Garter st Border of Strap above turning ridge at bottom of Bag and under Garter st Border at top of Bag. Work Overcast st around top of Bag and Pocket.

Weave I-Cord Drawstring through alternating Eyelets around top of Bag, beginning with hole at front of Bag (opposite side to joining of rnds). Tie bottom ends of I-Cord into knots.

Position Pocket on Strap so top of Pocket is 7" from top of Strap. Sew side and edges of Pocket to Strap using Overcast st.

Sew bottom edge of Strap to back side of Bag just above turning ridge. Sew top edge of Strap to Bag just under Garter st Border. Fold Strap up 1" from this top seam and sew folded edge to Bag just above Eyelet rnd.

Using yarn needle, weave in all loose ends.

Blocking: Use individual paper towel rolls (still in plastic wrapping) to stuff the length of Bag. Set this column on floor upside-down and gently stretch the bottom of the bag until rounded into the paper towel rolls. Spray with water until damp and leave to dry.

exercises
FOR KNITTERS

We knitters can labor for hours at a time,

under self-imposed pressure, with no breaks other than to turn the work at the end of a row. This can lead to aches and pains in our fingers, wrists, and arms. You can minimize these aches and pains dramatically, if you are mindful of your body and take a few moments each time you knit to recharge it. To help us all, I asked Maria Leone, a Pilates instructor and the daughter of one of my customers, for these useful exercises.

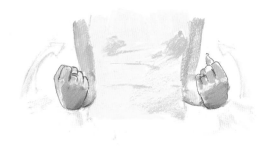

FOREARM STRETCH
Start seated upright feet firmly planted on the ground. Push one hand forward as if signaling "stop" with the elbow straight. With your opposite hand gently pull your fingertips back towards you. Hold 30 seconds, breathing deeply. Repeat with other hand.

YARN WINDER
Same start as Forearm Stretch. Allow your upper arm to hang free by your trunk. Bend your elbows so that your forearm is now parallel to the ground. Make fists with your hands and circle your wrists 5 times each direction.

CHEST STRETCH

Same start as Forearm Stretch. Reach both arms forward slightly lower than shoulder height and spread your fingers, palms wide, as if balancing a skein of yarn. Without dropping the skein, slowly open your arms, palms up, and reach diagonally behind you. Make sure your ribcage does not shift forward. Stop when you feel a stretch in the front of the shoulder and chest. Repeat 5 times.

NECK STRETCH

Same start as Forearm Stretch. Without bending your torso or tilting your shoulders, allow your head to lower to one side as if wearing a very heavy earring. Keep the opposite shoulder pulling down towards the floor. With gentle pressure, use one hand to increase the stretch. Hold 30 seconds. Repeat on other side.

SHOULDER OPENER

Same start as Forearm Stretch. Clasp your hands together and bring them behind your head. Open your elbows and pull your shoulder blades tight together. Hold for 5 seconds and repeat 5 times.

REACH FOR THE CASHMERE

Stretch both hands over your head. Pretending you are pulling a thick cashmere strand towards you, stretch one hand over the other. It's hard to reach, so allow your body to shift from side to side as your really reach for the cashmere.

CABLE STITCH STRETCH

Seated as above with the spine as long as possible. Keep your hips anchored in one spot as you rotate the upper body and head behind you. Use your arms to gently enhance the stretch and help you sit more upright. Keep your abdominals pulling into your spine. Hold 30 seconds. Repeat other side.

MARIA'S TIPS FOR

the perfect knitting pose

1 Make sure your position provides as much back support as possible. If you are seated in a very deep chair, use throw pillows to fill the gap between your lower spine and the back support. This will help to keep you more upright.

2 If you are comfortable, try to position yourself with both feet flat on the floor. Avoid crossed leg positions as much as possible (they are bad for your lower back), but if you must cross your legs, change your position frequently.

3 Make sure you are allowing your elbows to be heavy and hang by the sides of the body. If possible, use arm rests or throw pillows to support the lower arms.

4 Don't hold your neck tight. Allow your upper body to stay relaxed as your lower arms work.

special techniques

Backward Loop CO: With working yarn, make a loop (using slipknot) and place on right-hand needle [first st CO], *wind yarn around thumb clockwise, insert right-hand needle into front of loop on thumb, remove thumb and tighten st on needle; repeat from * for remaining sts to be CO, or for casting on at end of a row in progress.

Cable CO: With working yarn, make a loop (using a slipknot) and place on right-hand needle [first st CO], knit into slipknot, draw up a loop but do not drop st from left-hand needle; place new loop on left-hand needle; *insert tip of right-hand needle into space between last 2 sts on left-hand needle and draw up a loop; place loop on left-hand needle. Repeat from * for remaining sts to be CO, or for casting on at the end of a row in progress.

Crab Stitch (Reverse Single Crochet): Working from left to right, insert hook into next stitch, yarn over and draw up a loop; yarn over and draw it through both loops on hook.

Elastic BO: *Knit 2 sts together loosely through back loops; 1 st remains on right-handle needle. Slip stitch from right-hand needle to the left-hand needle, making sure it is not twisted. Repeat from * until required number of sts are bound off.

Fringe: Using number of strands required in pattern, fold in half; with RS of piece facing, insert crochet hook just above edge to receive fringe, from back to front; catch folded strands

of yarn with hook and pull through work to form a loop, insert ends of yarn through loop and pull to tighten.

Garter Stitch: Knit every row when working straight; knit 1 round, purl 1 round when working circular.

I-Cord: Using a double-pointed needle, cast on or pick up required number of sts; working yarn will be at left-hand side of the needle. * Transfer needle with sts to your left hand, bring yarn around behind work to right-hand side; using a second double-pointed needle, knit sts from right to left, pulling yarn from left to right for the first st; do not turn. Slide sts to opposite end of needle; repeat from * until cord is desired length. *Note: After a few rows, the tubular shape will become apparent.*

Kitchener Stitch: Hold pieces to be joined WS's together, with needles parallel, both ends pointing in same direction. Working from right to left, using yarn needle (yn) and yarn 4 times length of section to be joined, insert yn into first st on front needle (N1) purlwise, pull yarn through, leaving st on needle; insert yn into first st on back needle (N2) knitwise, pull yarn through, leaving st on needle; *insert yn into first st on N1 knitwise, pull yarn through, remove st from needle; insert yn into next st on N1 purlwise, pull yarn through, leave st on needle; insert yn into first st on N2 purlwise, pull yarn through, remove st from needle; insert yn into next st on N2 knitwise, pull yarn through, leave st on needle. Repeat from *, adjusting tension of sts as you go to match pieces being joined.

When 1 st remains on each needle, cut yarn and pass through last 2 sts to fasten off.

Knit-On CO: With working yarn, make a loop (using a slipknot) and place on the left-hand needle [first st CO], *knit into st on left-hand needle, draw up a loop but do not drop st from left-hand needle; place new loop on left-hand needle; repeat from * for remaining sts to be CO, or for casting on at end of a row in progress.

Outline Stitch BO: Break off yarn, leaving a long tail (approximately 12" for every 10 sts to be BO); thread tail onto yarn needle. With RS facing, tail at left and above work, * insert needle into second st from left as if to knit and into first st as if to purl; pull yarn through and slip first st off needle. Repeat from * until all sts have been bound off, keeping tension fairly loose; it may be tightened later.

Picot Point CO: Using Cable CO method, CO 3 sts. BO 2 sts; slip rem st back to left-hand needle. This makes one picot point. *CO 2 sts. BO 2 sts; slip rem st back to left-hand needle. Rep from * until you've worked one picot point for each CO st required in pattern, leaving final st on right-hand needle. Working from right to left across chain, beginning with second picot point, with right-hand needle, *pick up 1 st in horizontal bar above picot point; rep from * to end of chain. You now have required number of sts on right-hand needle. Turn, ready to work a WS row.

SPECIAL TECHNIQUES (CONTINUED)

Pompom: Use a pompom maker or the following method: Cut 2 cardboard circles to diameter of pompom desired. Cut 1" diameter hole in center of each circle. Cut small wedge out of each circle to allow for wrapping yarn. Hold circles together with openings aligned. Wrap yarn tightly around circles. Carefully cut yarn around outer edge of circles. Wrap 12" length of yarn around strands between circles and tie tightly. Slip circles off completed pompom; trim pompom but leave end of tie untrimmed and use to attach pompom to project.

Provisional CO: Using waste yarn, CO required number of sts; work in St st for 3-4 rows; work 1 row with a thin, smooth yarn (crochet cotton or ravel cord used for machine knitting) as a separator; change to main yarn and continue as directed. When ready to work live stitches, pull out separator row, placing live stitches on spare needle.

Provisional (Crochet Chain) CO: Using crochet hook and smooth yarn (crochet cotton or ravel cord used for machine knitting), work a crochet chain with a few more chains than the number of stitches needed; fasten off. If desired, tie knot on fastened-off end to mark end you will be unraveling from later. Turn chain over; with a needle one size smaller than required for piece and working yarn, starting a few chains in from beginning of chain, pick up and knit 1 st in each bump at back of chain, leaving any extra chains at end unworked. Change to needle size required for project on first row. When ready to work live stitches, unravel chain by loosening fastened-off end and "unzipping," placing live stitches on spare needle.

Ribbing: Although rib stitch patterns use different numbers of stitches, all are worked in same way, whether straight [in rows] or in-the-round. Instructions will specify how many sts to knit or purl; the example below uses k1, p1.

Row/Rnd 1: * K1, p1; repeat from * across, (end k1 if an odd number of stitches).

Row/Rnd 2: Knit the knit stitches and purl the purl stitches as they face you. Repeat Row/Rnd 2 for rib st.

Stockinette Stitch (St st): Knit on RS rows, purl on WS rows when working straight; knit every round when working in the round.

Three-Needle BO: Place sts to be joined onto two same-size needles; hold pieces to be joined with right sides facing each other and needles parallel, both pointing in same direction (to the right). Holding both needles in left hand, using working yarn and a third needle same size or one size larger, insert third needle into first st on front needle, then into first st on back needle; knit these 2 sts together; * knit next st from each needle together (2 sts on right-hand needle); pass first st over second st to BO 1 st. Repeat from * until 1 st remains on third needle; cut yarn and fasten off.

abbreviations

BO – Bind off

CC – Contrast color

Circ – Circular

CO – Cast on

Dpn – Double-pointed needle(s)

K – Knit

K2tog – Knit 2 sts together.

K1b – Insert right-hand needle through top right side of st one row below next st on left-hand needle. Place st on left-hand needle without twisting and knit it as normal.

K1-f/b – Knit into front loop and back loop of same st to increase 1 st.

K1-tbl – Knit 1 through back loop

MC – Main color

M1 or m1-l (make 1-left slanting) – With tip of left-hand needle inserted from front to back, lift strand between 2 needles onto left-hand needle; knit strand through back loop to increase 1 st.

M1-p (make 1 purlwise) - With tip of left-hand needle inserted from back to front, lift strand between 2 needles onto left-hand needle; purl strand through front loop to increase 1 st.

M1-p-l (make 1 purlwise-left slanting) – With tip of left-hand needle inserted from front to back, lift strand between 2 needles onto left-hand needle; purl strand through back loop to increase 1 st.

M1-r (make 1-right slanting) – With tip of left-hand needle inserted from back to front, lift strand between 2 needles onto left-hand needle; knit it through front loop to increase 1 st.

P – Purl

P1-f/b – Purl next st through front of its loop, then through back of its loop, to increase 1 st.

Pm – Place marker

Psso (pass slipped stitch over) – Pass slipped stitch on right-hand needle over sts indicated in instructions, as in binding off.

Rnd – Round

RS – Right side

Sc (single crochet) – Insert hook into next st and draw up a loop (2 loops on hook), yarn over and draw through both loops on hook.

Skp (slip one stitch, knit one stitch, pass slip st over knit stitch) – Slip 1 st knitwise, then knit next st. Insert left needle into front of slipped st. Pass slipped st over knit st and off right needle.

Sl (slip) – Slip stitch(es) as if to purl, unless otherwise specified.

Sl st (crochet slip stitch) – Insert hook in next st (or st specified), yarn over hook, and draw through loop on hook.

Sl 1-k2tog-psso (slip 1 st, k2 sts together, pass slipped st over k2tog) – Slip 1 st knitwise, then knit next 2 sts together. Insert left needle into front of slipped st. Pass slipped st over the k2tog and off right needle.

Sm – Slip marker

Ssk (slip, slip, knit) – Slip next 2 sts to right-hand needle one at a time as if to knit; return them back to left-hand needle one at a time in their new orientation; knit them together through back loop(s).

St(s) – Stitch(es)

K1-tbl – Knit 1 st through back loop, twisting st.

Tbl – Through back loop

Tog – Together

WS – Wrong side

wyib – With yarn in back

wyif – With yarn in front

yb – Yarn back

yf – Yarn front

Yo – Yarnover

sources for supplies

Contact these suppliers to find local sources for all of the yarns used in the projects in this book:

BLUE SKY ALPACAS, INC
PO Box 88
Cedar, MN 55011
888 460 8862
www.blueskyalpacas.com

CLASSIC ELITE YARNS
122 Western Ave.
Lowell, MA 01851
978 453 2837
www.classiceliteyarns.com

FIESTA YARNS
5401 San Diego NE
Albuquerque, NM 87113
505 892 5008
www.fiestayarns.com

KNIT ONE, CROCHET TOO, INC
91 Tandberg Trail, Unit 6
Windham, ME 04062
207 892 9625
www.knitonecrochettoo.com

KNITTING FEVER, INC
PO Box 336
315 Bayview Ave.
Amityville, NY 11701
516 546 3600
www.knittingfever.com

KOIGU WOOL DESIGNS
PO Box 158
Chatsworth, ON
Canada N0H 1G0
888 765 WOOL
www.koigu.com

LANA GROSSA
(see Muench Yarns)

MANOS DEL URUGUAY
Fairmount Fibers
915 N. 28th St.
Philadelphia, PA 19130
888 566 9970
www.fairmountfibers.com

MISTI INTERNATIONAL, INC
PO Box 2532
Glen Ellyn, IL 60138
888 776 YARN
www.mistialpaca.com

MUENCH YARNS, INC
1323 Scott St.
Petaluma, CA 94954
800 733 9276
www.muenchyarns.com

RIO DE LA PLATA YARNS
13101 W. Washington Blvd.
Suite 139
Los Angeles, CA 90066
800 972 0722
www.riodelaplatayarns.com

ROWAN YARNS
Westminster Fibers, Inc.
165 Ledge St.
Nashua, NH 03060
800 445 9276
www.westminsterfibers.com

TAHKI * STACY CHARLES, INC
70 – 30 80th St.
Building 36
Ridgewood, NY 11385
800 338 YARN
www.tahkistacycharles.com

TRENDSETTER YARNS
16745 Saticoy St.
Suite 101
Van Nuys, CA 91406
818 780 5497
www.trendsetteryarns.com

TWISTED SISTERS KNITTING
www.twistedsistersknitting.com

contributors

BETH ABARAVICH

Beth teaches knitting, fashion illustration, and eveningwear design at Otis College of Art and Design, in addition to taking care of her beloved husband and daughter.

MARY-HEATHER COGAR

Mary-Heather worked as my trusted store manager and so much more while I was writing this book. She was my sounding board, my confidant, the youthful ying to my a-little-older-than-youthful yang. Visit her website at www.rainyday.squarespace.com

KAT COYLE

One day a couple of years ago Kat came into my store wearing a very beautiful mohair lace shawl and I immediately commissioned her to knit me one of her designs to wear to a black-tie event. Through that experience I became familiar with her beautiful knitting and paintings and her overall design aesthetic. When she is not whipping up mohair confections, she is busy being mom to her little Felix. Visit her website at www.katcoyle.com.

TERRY CUPURJIA

Terri is co-owner of Twisted Sisters, a California-based yarn studio. Together, she and her partner hand-dye and handpaint yarns and design patterns to go with them. Visit their website at www.twistedsistersknitting.com.

KATHERINE LEE

After finishing engineering school and earning a master's degree in business administration, Katherine decided to found her own knitwear design company in Los Angeles, where she lives with her husband and children. Visit her website at www.sweaterbabe.com.

HELENE ROUX

Helene has been knitting since she was a little girl in Cannes, France, and now sells her own designs. I am always drawn to her playful sense of color.

ULLI SCHOBER SHIBUYA

Ulli is a makeup artist for fashion and advertising photography. She is constantly on the go but is never without her knitting. She grew up in Austria where knitting became second nature to her at a very early age. She is one of those people who designs her projects while they're on her needles – never working from a pattern.

JUDY SPECTOR

Judy is a registered nurse. When she isn't overseas teaching patients allergy and asthma management techniques, she teaches knitting in Los Angeles.

JULIA TRICE

I first noticed Julia when she was slouched across the big orange chair at the store, knitting Alice Starmore's Kilronnan (a very complicated cabled sweater) and talking with a friend about a legal case she was working on. I immediately fell in love with her dry sense of humor and was blown away by her knitting skills. After much begging, I was able to convince her to moonlight at Knit Cafe a couple of evenings a week. Visit her website at www.mindofwinter.prettyposies.com.

JENNY WHITE

Jenny, whom I affectionately call Whippersnapper, was a relatively new knitter when I met her. But there she was with her ponytail high on her head, confidently cutting a finger off her Koigu glove, which was still on the needles, while firmly instructing both of her younger sisters how to do increases on their projects. I hired her to work at Knit Cafe immediately.

DEENA WILLIAMS

Deena has been an avid knitter for three years. She now designs a line of stylish, high-quality products to help knitters organize their lives. Visit her website at www.knitcouture.com.

acknowledgments

Jolie

Nicole

Ngyuen (left)
Amira (below)

Joe, the UPS guy

Komari

Judy

Todd

Sierra

Mary-Heather and me

Beverly

(from left to right) Crystal, Jamie, Vicky, and Hope

Lilly and Charlie

It makes a huge difference to have talented and supportive people in your corner, people who really get who you are and what you're trying to accomplish.

I would like to thank all of you from the bottom of my heart.

Melanie Falick, who taught me that there is a right way and a wrong way to fly a trapeze. Thank you for being my safety net.

Victoria Pearson, whose beautiful photographs make me smile.

Sasha Emerson, for helping me to create this place I love so much.

My dear friend Lilly Tartikoff, who taught me to always take the high road.

Mary-Heather Cogar, who was my sounding board, trusted confidant, and store manager while I was writing this book.

My wonderful and spirited models: Todd Barrett, Jacob Browne, Komari Crisp, Mary-Heather Cogar, Nicole Forester, Crystal Freeman, Judy Greer, Vicky Huxtable, Jolie Jenkins, Jamie Mackta, Charlie Mischer, Heather Mischer, Lilly Mischer, Jenny Mischer, Amira Orange, Ngyuen Orange, Beverly Sassoon, Hope Anita Smith, and Sierra Strickland.

My tireless and enthusiastic knitters: Denise Bouter, Debbie Harper, Eadie Kleiman, Megan Kellie, Jamie Mackta, Helene Roux, Hope Anita Smith, and Daniel Thornton.

My beloved Knit Cafe family. Please forgive me for not naming each of you individually, but there just isn't enough paper! You are the heart and soul of Knit Cafe and you are the reason I love to go to work every day!

The Knit Cafe Kids' Club regulars: Sophie, Jordan, Molly, Amira, Elena, Julie, Joey, Ally, Allegra, Sydney, Emily, Isabelle, and Jaimie. Your energy and smiles light up the room whenever you're around.

My accountant, Alan Reback, and my tough-as-nails bookkeeper, Portia Qualls.

Joe, the UPS guy (self-explanatory).

Trenese, our favorite mail carrier.

I would also like to thank Erica Courtney, Jane Lockhart, Peter Tigler, the Traditional Equitation School, Joanie Berkeley Floral Designs, Valerie's Confections, Michelle Reiner, Tamasin Reid, Fi Campbell-Johnson, Luisa Ayon, Amelya Freeman, SQGNH, Tina Gianesini, Sarah Von Dreele, Andrea Glickson, Melody Meyer, Sue McCain, and Jan McCarthy.

My children, Charlie and Lilly, who are two of the nicest people I've ever known. Their support, encouragement, and sometimes brutal honesty truly touch me every day.

Lastly, I want to thank my husband, Don Mischer, who not only expertly wore his husband, friend, and provider hat so that I could write this book, but also wore his Mr. Mom hat with an agility that makes me green with envy.

index